THE MIDDLE AGES

Published in 1996 by
Marshall Cavendish Corporation
99 White Plains Road
Tarrytown, NY 10591-9001
U.S.A.

Editor: Henk Dijkstra
Executive Editor: Paulien Retèl
Revision Editor: Hans Scheurkogel (The Frankish Empire, Charlemagne,
The Western Empire, Feudalism, The Feudal Society,
Early Medieval Politics, The Muslims, The Reconquista, The Crusades),
Henk Singor (Byzantium, The Middle Byzantine Empire)
Art Director: Henk Oostenrijk, Studio 87, Utrecht, The Netherlands
Index Editors: Schuurmans & Jonkers, Leiden, The Netherlands
Preface: Leslie Bussis Tait, Ph.D., Adjunct Professor, Art History,
The Bard Graduate Center for Studies in the Decorative Arts, New York City

The History of the Ancient and Medieval World is a completely revised and
updated edition *of The Adventure of Mankind.*
©1996 by Marshall Cavendish Corporation, Tarrytown, New York, and
HD Communication Consultants BV, Hilversum,
The Netherlands

Library of Congress Cataloging-in-Publication Date

History of the ancient and medieval world / edited by Henk Dijkstra.
p. cm.
Completely rev. and updated ed. of: The Adventure of mankind (second edition 1995).
Contents: —v.9. The Middle Ages.
ISBN 0-7614-0360-4 (v.9).— ISBN 0-7614-0351-5 (lib.bdg.:set)
1. History, Ancient—Juvenile literature. 2. Middle Ages—History—Juvenile literature. I. Dijkstra, Henk. II. Title: Adventure of mankind
D117.H57 1996
930—dc20/95-35715

History of the Ancient & Medieval World

Volume 9

The Middle Ages

Marshall Cavendish
New York   Toronto   Sydney

The Middle Ages

Reliquary of the emperor Otto III

CONTENTS

1158 Preface

1159 The Frankish Empire
Western Europe in the Middle Ages

1165 Charlemagne
Charles the Great, Ruler of the West

1177 The Western Empire
Christendom as a Rule

1189 Feudalism
A System of Lords and Serfs

1201 The Feudal Society
The Structure of the Empire

1213 Early Medieval Politics
Secular Rulers and Papal Power

1225 The Muslims
Rule in Spain

1231 The Reconquista
The Recovery of the West

1243 Byzantium
The Christian Stronghold in the East

1255 The Middle Byzantine Empire
Still the Center of the World

1267 The Crusades
Wars in the Name of God

1279 Time Line

1285 Glossary

1289 Bibliography and Further Reading

1290 Illustration Credits

1291 Index

Preface

From the sixth through the eleventh centuries, power struggles raged between and among political and religious forces of Western and Eastern Europe and the Middle East. This period began with great migrations. The Magyars and Huns swept into Western Europe, as the Vikings moved south from Scandinavia. The Muslims in the seventh and eighth centuries spread east to Asia and west to the Iberian Peninsula. In the eleventh century there was movement in other directions, as Christian armies launched the Reconquista in Spain and the Crusades in the East.

In the midst of these power struggles, the Franks steadily achieved greater political power in the West, beginning with Charlemagne and continuing through the Ottonians who would rule as Holy Roman Emperors. Faced with invasion from the Lombards in the eighth century, the pope requested aid from the Frankish king. In return for military protection, the pope sanctioned the Carolingian line. On Christmas Day 800, Pope Leo III crowned Charlemagne as Ruler of the Roman Empire. By allowing the secular title to be dependent on papal approval, the Carolingians set a precedent that would have serious consequences for church and state relations throughout the Middle Ages.

As the geographically separate spheres of Christendom developed, liturgical and theological differences emerged in the Greek-speaking East and the Latin-speaking West. The pope in Rome claimed primacy over patriarchs of the Eastern Church. Differing interpretations of church doctrine and liturgy led to the Great Schism of 1054. A key difference was the role of icons in religious practices.

The representation of religious subjects formed an important part of church decoration in the West and the East from the early Christian period. In the Byzantine church, however, icons or holy images came to be venerated as part of regular practice.

This attitude disturbed certain fundamental religious leaders as well as Byzantine emperors who felt threatened by this practice. The period of iconoclasm (726 to 843) saw the destruction of much religious art. Ultimately, the practice of venerating images was restored.

In the realm of art and culture, Charlemagne was keenly interested in reviving antiquity. Artists at his court actively copied late antique manuscripts and ivories, and his builders brought actual elements of late antique buildings from Rome and Ravenna to his palace in Aachen. There was much admiration in the West for the sumptuous luxury and lavish court rituals of the East. Artists of Byzantium were regarded as preservers of the classical artistic traditions.

In light of Charlemagne's concern with reviving antique learning and culture, his war against the Iberian Muslims is not without irony. The Muslims conserved and continued much of the Helleno-Roman philosophical and scientific heritage lost in Western Europe. Many antique texts were unknown in the West until they were translated late in the twelfth or thirteenth centuries from Arabic. Culture flourished in the Muslim cities. The Reconquista grew as a movement of the Christian kingdoms unified to reconquer the Iberian Peninsula from Muslim domination.

From the 1070s the Byzantine Empire suffered terrible defeats from the Muslims. This weakened position prompted them to summon Christians of Western Europe for assistance in reclaiming lost territory that included Christianity's most holy city, Jerusalem. When Pope Urban II rallied the First Crusade in 1095, a series of crusades followed that engaged Christian and Muslim armies over the next two centuries.

Leslie Bussis Tait, Ph.D.
Adjunct Professor, Art History
The Bard Graduate Center
for Studies in the Decorative Arts,
New York City

EXCELSA VOCE

The Frankish Empire

Western Europe in the Middle Ages

Under Frankish law promulgated by Clovis shortly before his death, no distinction was made between public and private individuals, a fact that was to have far-reaching political effect. The rules of inheritance demanded that any legacy be divided among the sons of the deceased. They applied to king and landowner alike. It was hard enough to settle an ordinary inheritance, let alone the kingdom and the

Merovingian dynasty Clovis had founded. When he died in Paris in AD 511, his empire had to be divided among his sons, who soon took to armed conflict. The empire rapidly disintegrated.

No individual Merovingian ultimately triumphed in the battles that followed. Clovis's grip on power had already been weakened by prolonged war before his death. During the century that followed,

1159

divided imperial power faced a challenging aristocracy. As the empire declined, the Frankish elite prospered, happy to accept Merovingian gifts and concessions while paying less and less regard to erstwhile royal power. The outposts of the empire fell first. In Aquitaine, Bavaria, and Brittany, local lords took over. By the end of the century, there was no single Frankish Empire. A number of vying sub-kingdoms had arisen in its place.

Wealth Equals Land

The use of money, together with trade, gradually declined in the Frankish economy. Each region and each rural estate was forced to become completely self-sufficient, producing what its own inhabitants needed. Wealth was figured in terms of land, not money. The man with the most land could produce the most and was therefore the richest and most powerful.

This situation was reinforced by the existing system of farm production. The large landowners did not work the land themselves. They had tenant farmers, dependents who worked the farms and gave the owners a share of the harvest in return for protection. This released the landowners from the production process, allowing them time for administrative tasks and leisure.

A small group of wealthy landowners, in effect, ran the empire. Most important among them was the king. He owned not only the greatest number and the largest of the rural estates but had these holdings spread throughout his entire domain. He could maintain his personal authority simply by moving from place to place. The practice was justified by the fact that the king was expected to pay for his reign out of his own pocket.

By the end of the eighth century, from the viewpoint of the landowners, the economic situation took a turn for the better. Royal prerogatives were not maintained and the pattern of ownership visibly altered. Actual power came to rest increasingly with the second category of large landowners, the aristocracy. A third category eventually was formed by the religious institutions: the abbeys, the bishoprics, and others. Leading positions in the church were typically in the hands of members of either aristocratic or royal families.

Gold disk fibula (pin) of a Frankish nobleman from the time of Pépin of Herstal (c. 680)

The Mayors of the Palace (Major Domus)

The power of a Merovingian king rested on his personal prestige as well as his wealth. He acquired that prestige in part through lineage, his descent from the royal family of Clovis, but his reputation as an administrator was at least as important a factor. The appearance of managerial skill was paramount. Yet, in fact, only two things were actually expected of a king: protecting the people of his empire and expanding its frontiers.

The royal role in administration was gradually taken over in each subkingdom by the major domus (mayor of the palace). The kings after about AD 650 are known as *rois fainéants* or "good-for-nothing kings."

Seventh-century gold coin with a portrait of Dagobert I, the last true Merovingian king. After his rule the majordomos effectively assumed power.

By the middle of the seventh century, the power of the Franks over the empire was restricted to the area north of the Loire. Two Frankish kingdoms existed there, side by side: Neustria, in the northwest of Clovis's former empire, and Austrasia, in the northeast. Each kingdom was run by a *major domus* intent on subjugating the other. Pépin of Herstal, the mayor of Austrasia, defeated his Neustrian counterpart at Testry in 687. This put both territories of the Frankish kingdom under the hegemony of the mayor Pépin, a decisive blow to royal authority.

From then on, this mayoral dynasty (eventually to be called the Carolingians after its most famous son, Charlemagne) claimed a growing share of the erstwhile royal prerogatives of protection and expansion. Pépin himself went after the Frisians, north of Austrasia. Convincingly defeating their king, he reoccupied the old stronghold of Utrecht.

Pépin combined what he saw as his primary task of expansion with another activity, support for the church. Missionaries entered the newly conquered areas to bring the god of the new ruler to his people. Although certainly acting out of personal conviction in his religious zeal, Pépin undoubtedly also recognized the political profit to be gained. Maintaining an image as a pillar of the church, he was well aware that universal conversion to Christianity would consolidate his conquest at the same time.

Pépin did not use Frankish missionaries, but Anglo-Saxons who had converted to Christianity relatively recently, in the seventh century. Precisely for this reason, clergymen there were strongly convinced of the validity of Christian doctrine and committed to the conversion effort. Of particular significance here is the fact that the Anglo-Saxons were converted on the initiative of the pope. Anglo-Saxon priests were the only ones during this period recognizing papal spiritual authority. They would foster the subsequent contact between the pope and the Carolingians.

The Hammer

Pépin the Short of Herstal died in 714, passing on power to his illegitimate son Charles, who carried on his father's policies of reasserting Frankish predominance. Rebelling lords soon came up against the young majordomo's military talent. His subjects nicknamed him *martel*, or "the hammer." The church did very well by Charles Martel. It generally supported the mayors in the hope of gaining the protec-

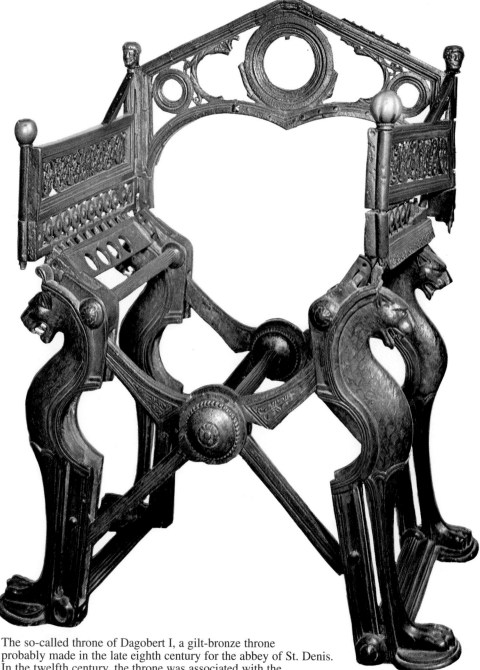

The so-called throne of Dagobert I, a gilt-bronze throne probably made in the late eighth century for the abbey of St. Denis. In the twelfth century, the throne was associated with the seventh-century King Dagobert, believed to have been the founder of the monastery who ruled from 602 to 639. The throne is collapsible, so that the king could take it with him when he traveled.

Eighth-century gold coin inscribed with the name of Pépin the Short

1161

Miniature from a fifteenth-century manuscript which shows Charles Martel (*right*) leading his army into battle against the Muslim army of 'Abd al-Raḥmān

tion from them that it could no longer expect from the royal Merovingians.

It was not long before Charles was able to devote attention to his foreign ambitions. He had two points of expansion in mind: the area on the far side of the Rhine in the north and Italy. The north and east offered the best chances at first. He defeated the Frisians in the Rhine delta, where the conquests of Pépin had been lost during the changeover of power. Here, too, the son followed in his father's footsteps, but Charles's activities stretched over a much greater area. The Anglo-Saxon missionaries were able to continue his work, consolidating his victories through conversion of the people to Christianity. He waged war on the Saxons, the Thuringians, the Alemannians, and the Bavarians, overall expanding Frankish presence in Germany and uniting the realm under his authority.

The Establishment of Fiefdoms

Meanwhile, the Muslims in Spain had also been seeking new conquests. Their cavalry periodically crossed the Pyrenees into Aquitaine to carry out raids. Charles saw his chance to carry out the other royal task, protection.

Fifteenth-century miniature showing the battle Pépin the Short waged to capture the city of Narbonne from the Muhammadan in 759. Clothing and armor, however, were completely different in the eighth century than the artist depicts here and in the above illustration.

He did so with resounding success in 732 at the battle of Poitiers. The Muslim cavalry was smashed to pieces on a wall of Franks. Charles's foot soldiers had saved his regime. Nevertheless, the ability of the enemy cavalry had made a strong impression on him. Charles decided to revise Frankish military strategy, a decision of great economic significance.

At the time, the infantry was the most important division in the army. Every free man had the right to be a soldier under his lord, but only the richest could afford the equipment necessary to be a cavalry officer. Charles Martel thought this had to be changed but recognized the enormity of the undertaking. He would have to increase the number of people in the wealthy class. That would mean making land available to them, even large estates. He decided to seize these lands from the church, claiming territory on a large scale, "in the name of the king," in order to carry out his plan.

This innovation would powerfully strengthen the position of the Carolingians. Charles did not give out the requisite land-ownership but granted it in fief. He required the new estate owner to swear allegiance to him. He augmented the old aristocracy with a group of newcomers who were entirely dependent upon him for their position.

The battle-weary Charles died in 741. He had made it clear on all fronts that he was more than capable of carrying out the tasks intended for a king. He did not consider royal lineage essential, regarding himself powerful enough to leave the throne vacant after the death of the last of the Merovingians. Nor did he regard the church as omnipotent, clearly able to use church lands for his own purposes without encountering any significant opposition. His importance to history, however, lies in his concept of the fiefdom. His policy of granting large estates in return for an oath of loyalty formed the basis of the feudal system which would govern European political organization in the centuries that followed.

The estate and the authority of Charles Martel was divided upon his death between his two sons Pépin and Carloman, in accordance with law. At first they worked harmoniously together, but after a few years, Carloman gave full power to Pépin and withdrew to a monastery. Pépin promptly removed Carloman's sons from government, to the advantage of his own, and called the lords of the Frankish Empire together in council. They deposed the last Merovingian, putting an end to the dynasty, and elected Pépin king in 751.

This was preceded by a letter Pépin had written to the Pope Zacharias asking, according to a contemporary historian, "whether it was right that those who were of royal lineage and were called kings but had no power in their kingdoms should

Manuscript from the abbey of St. Denis in France. The illustration shows Dagobert I, who built an abbey on the site where St. Denis was buried.

ed another alliance by reluctantly agreeing to marry the daughter of the Lombardian King Desiderius. The wedding was hardly over before the pope's opinion became known. He described the marriage as "the work of the devil, an utterly illegal union, something insane, through which the superior Frankish blood would be polluted by the stinking faithless race of the Lombards from which, as everyone knew, the race of lepers was descended." Charlemagne sent his new bride back to Italy, but for what

Miniature (probably from fifteenth or sixteenth century) from the eleventh-century epic poem *Reinoud of Montalbaen*, which treats the noblemen's unsuccessful rebellion against Charlemagne.

combination of personal and political reasons is uncertain.

The strong language of Rome's bishop was not simply the product of religious indignation. The highly independent Lombard king, indeed no Christian, was showing great interest in the papal territories.

Carloman died suddenly in 771. Charlemagne, permitting no opposition from his nephews, declared himself sole king. The widow fled with her children to King Desiderius, who now broke ties with Charlemagne and asked Pope Adrian I, successor to Stephen II, to anoint the sons of Carloman as kings. This forced Charlemagne to the assistance of the pope.

Charlemagne crossed the Alps with an army and, besieging their capital Pavia, defeated the Lombards there. His potential rivals, his nephews, disappeared. In contrast to Pépin, he put an end to Lombard independence, deposing Desiderius. He declared himself the Lombard king and appointed Frankish lords to make sure his new subjects were obedient. In 774, before the siege was even over, Charlemagne celebrated Easter in St. Peter's Basilica in Rome and promised the pope restoration of his ancient rights and worldly territory. In fact, he only handed over small holdings to papal authority and retained full sovereignty over the Lombard kingdom.

The Saxons

Now Charlemagne could turn to other conquests, old and new. In 772, he had retaliated against Saxon attacks along the Rhine. Now he set out to bring that pagan tribe, stubbornly clinging to its own independence, into his Christian kingdom. The Saxons turned out to be formidable opponents. Throughout their entire history, they had never submitted to a ruler. Freemen, they had always managed to defend the independence of their villages, uniting in loose federation only in the face of greatest danger. The war would last more than thirty years, coordinated by the fierce warrior Widukind who used successful guerrilla tactics in the great forests of Europe. Frankish strategy had no real answer to this, often resorting to senseless massacre. Between 775 and 777, Charlemagne mounted several campaigns against the Saxons that resulted in mass baptism (the alternative was death) and a treaty of allegiance signed at a diet (or convention) in Paderborn. When they rose again only a few years later, he considered it high treason and religious apostasy and responded with the mass execution of 4,500 Saxons in 782. Only exhaustion would ultimately force the afflicted Saxons to give up in 804. Charlemagne resettled much of the population in Frankish or Frisian areas to break any final resistance, sending loyal Franks to occupy the abandoned estates in the subjugated Saxon lands.

Spain

At the close of the first decade of his rule, Charlemagne suffered his first defeat. At the diet in Paderborn, he agreed to enter Spain to assist some Arabs in a revolt against the Umayyad leader in Córdoba. The periodic Muslim cavalry raids out of Spain into Aquitaine were another factor in his decision. His intention was to establish

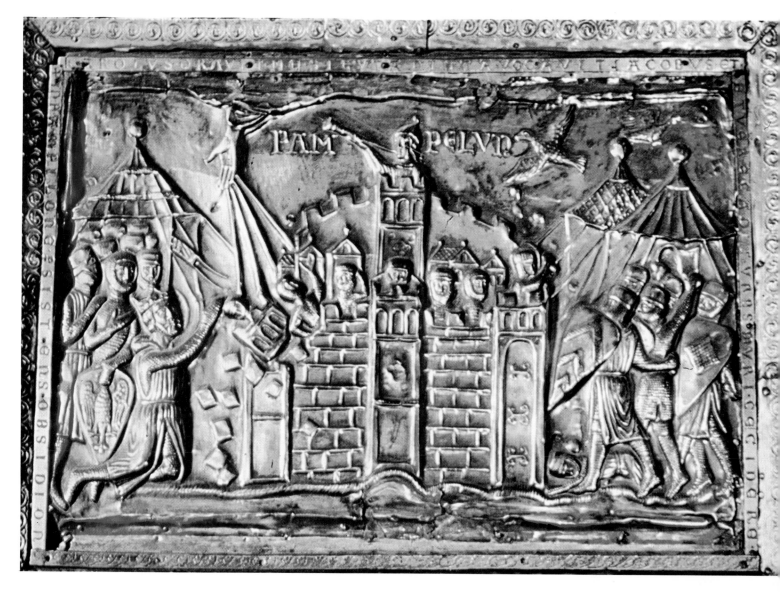

a military district south of the Pyrenees to serve as a buffer for the empire. This he succeeded in doing, forming a rather less than solid border province around Barcelona. He besieged Zaragoza but could not take the city. On the return journey over the Pyrenees, the entire rear guard of his army was caught in a Basque ambush. The commander Roland was killed. He would be immortalized in song and legend.

Germanic Tribes

Charlemagne's demand for unconditional subjugation began a series of cruel and bloody wars in which Germanic tribal freedom finally perished. He repeatedly had to pacify recently conquered areas, finding it difficult to consolidate the frontiers of his empire. The Bavarians and the Frisians, like the Saxons, refused to give up their traditional way of life. The murder of the great missionary Boniface and his followers in Frisian territory in 754 had already indicated their attitude toward subjugation.

The allies he acquired among the Germans frequently turned out to be untrustworthy.

In 788, with the deposing of his once-allied cousin, the Bavarian leader Duke Tassilo III, Charlemagne ended the notion of Germanic independence. He integrated the Christian Bavarians into the empire, together with the Alemanni and Thuringian tribes. Even after the death of Charlemagne, his successors had no need to fear revolts from these West German tribes or the Saxons. He had broken their power for good.

To the east of them, in the steppes of modern-day Hungary and Austria, Slavic peoples had founded principalities under the hegemony of the virtually invincible Avars. Charlemagne destroyed the Avar kingdom itself so completely that the Avars as a people disappeared from history. He made no attempt to subjugate their lands, contenting himself with imposing tribute on the Slavic principalities on his eastern borders without requiring even conversion.

Cover of a twelfth- or thirteenth-century silver reliquary, which shows the siege of the Spanish city of Pamplona by Charlemagne's army. The siege took place in 788 during Charlemagne's expedition against the Muhammadans in Spain.

The Making of an Emperor

Charlemagne now controlled most of western Europe as the only ruler in western Christendom. Contemporaries were forced to draw comparisons with the ancient Western Roman Empire now that their king ruled from the Ebro to the Elbe.

Section of a mosaic in the church of St. John Lateran in Rome. The apostle Paul hands Pope Leo III the *pallium* as a symbol of spiritual power and presents Charlemagne with a standard, a symbol of secular power.

Charlemagne was the equivalent of an emperor. Why not give him the title?

The office of the Roman emperor had acquired a sacred character over the course of time, symbolizing the unity of the church. After the imperial conversion to Christianity, every emperor was considered the head of all Christians and the protector of all believers, God's governor on Earth. Charlemagne, still only Frankish king, had proven himself capable of taking on this imperial role.

An iconoclastic emperor, successor to the Roman emperors, had ascended the throne of the Bronze Palace in Constantinople. People in Rome began to ask themselves whether that Byzantine emperor should hold his position. He was seen as betraying his holy mission, a heretic and an enemy of the faith. The ruler regarded himself as the sovereign of all Christians. He had never officially given up the lost provinces in the west and to him the Frankish kings were still a kind of lowly lords of the fuedal system. In practice, however, he awarded his allies distinguished Byzantine titles. Although these meant little to the Germanic rulers, the Eastern Roman Empire itself enjoyed great prestige. To the Goths, the Franks, and the Lombards, Constantinople was a faraway fantasy city told about in exaggerated stories of sophisticated Byzantine culture, huge armies, and a vast treasure of gold coins *(solidi)*.

In reality, the two empires were now vastly different. Iconoclasm and independence were both factors in that difference. The Western popes, still nominally subjects of the Eastern empire, had not only rejected Byzantium's iconoclastic theology and religious practice, they had moved to separate themselves politically from it. Papal documents then were dated from the reign of Charlemagne's father, King Pépin. (They would later be dated by papal reign.) The popes had established an autonomous region under Charlemagne's protection around Rome and Ravenna. Byzantium had essentially acquiesced to this Roman autonomy, asserting influence only on Sicily and in southern Italy.

A mysterious document was found that ostensibly legitimized the papal interest in that independence. Called the *donatio Constantini* (Donation or Blessing of Constantine), this is known today as the most famous forgery in history. Probably during Pope Adrian's reign, the forger composed the document in the style and wording of a Byzantine deed, purportedly written by Constantine the Great. In it, he grants the whole western part of his empire to the pope in Rome. The Donation would play an important role in the Middle Ages. For centuries, the Roman papacy would use it to justify its claim to the right of worldly supervision over the monarchs of Europe. The document's immediate international political implications must have been more important to Charlemagne.

Charlemagne played it both ways,

Ninth-century equestrian statue, possibly of Charlemagne. The emperor wears his crown and holds a globe in his hand as symbols of his worldly power.

The cathedral in Aachen, Germany, which Charlemagne built to serve as his palace chapel and where he lies buried. The church is octagonal and so similar to the San Vitale church in Ravenna. It was consecrated by Pope Leo III in 805.

Talisman of Charlemagne that, according to legend, was found by Otto III in Charlemagne's tomb. It contains a holy relic.

seeking the approval of both sides. He visited Rome again in 781, this time to have his sons Pépin and Louis anointed kings of the Lombards and the Aquitanians. He was also recognized as ruler by the Byzantine Empress Irene, mother of Constantine IV. That cordial understanding ended with his assault on Byzantium-held southern Italy in 787.

Emperor Charlemagne
In May 799, Pope Leo III was taken prisoner by the local lords staging a coup attempt. He managed to escape and flee over the Alps to his protector Charlemagne. The king had him safely escorted back to Rome. Charlemagne went to Rome himself in November 800. The pope went to meet him as was customary, but instead of the usual two miles, he went the full twelve miles distance laid down in protocol for the reception of an emperor. It was clear there was something in the air. Before the king and by a tribunal, Leo was acquitted of all charges presented by his enemies.

On Christmas Day, Charlemagne attended mass celebrated at St. Peter's Basilica by Leo. Like his father before him, the king held the Roman title *patricius Romanorum* (protector of the Romans). Leo now crowned him emperor. Charlemagne accepted the title but is said to have expressed surprise.

The Frankish historian Einhard quotes him as saying he would never have set foot in the Basilica had he known of the planned coronation. Yet it had been negotiated earlier. One interpretation is that the new emperor was simply expressing humility; another is that he did not want to be crowned on the initiative of the pope. Charlemagne already held dominion over the western part of the former Roman Empire. His coronation had no constitutional basis, yet it set the precedent for the medieval empire to follow and the linkage between the Franks and the Holy Roman Empire.

Byzantium reacted with great annoyance to his coronation. Empress Irene and her successor Nicephorus regarded their new counterpart as little more than a usurper. Charlemagne, in turn, threatened to stage a large-scale invasion of the Byzantine-controlled areas in southern Italy. In order to prove what he was capable of, he conquered the nominally Byzantine lagoon of Venice. With that area as security, he finally obtained recognition as emperor. That fact did not end the friction between the eastern and western emperors, for obvious reasons. The West had officially separated from the East, accentuating its independence with its own emperor and defender of the faithful. The split was incontrovertible.

Restoration of the Roman Empire?
In some sense, Pope Leo did not start a new chapter in history when he placed the emperor's crown on Charlemagne's head. Rather he drew on the heritage of Constantine. Charlemagne was not declared the emperor of the Franks; Leo crowned him emperor of the Holy Roman Empire, a logical consequence of Carolingian politics.

For generations, Carolingians had been expanding the borders of the Frankish Empire to include the whole of Latin Christendom. Now it appeared they had brought a new Roman Empire into existence. Charlemagne guided this hope of restoration, cherished by his subjects. He put himself at the head of a new movement to support the military power of his empire with a spiritual and cultural revival. He would need to develop the empire's legal and administrative mechanisms, as well.

The Court
As king, like previous Frankish royalty, Charlemagne had no single official permanent residence. He would travel from one imperial palace to another, depending on the season, taking his court with him, making political and legal decisions as he went.

Summers he often went with the army on military campaigns.

In 794, he decided to center the new empire around his palace in Aachen rather than Rome, where he had previously spent four months of the year. Determined to make it a worthy residence, he turned it into a center of art and culture. (Its walls would be built into a city hall in the fourteenth century.) He also had a church built there, borrowing ideas and materials from Rome and Ravenna, that still stands today.

The emperor's court was comprised of his family, the *capella* (clergy in personal service to him), and a number of temporal officials and educators. He wanted to make the court the leading force of the empire in matters of religion, culture, and education, while ruling the empire through it. It was the basis for both administration and justice.

The Assembly
A concomitant feature of Charlemagne's reign was the annual general assembly, held variously in core Frankish territory or one of the conquered regions. Here the court was joined by magistrates and nobles from all over the empire to hand down justice and to review all matters of importance, military and ecclesiastical as well as legal. The functions of church and state were by no means considered separate.

One of Charlemagne's most difficult problems was dealing with the nobility, an essential component of the assemblies. He had to have the assistance of the lords of the aristocracy in key administrative and political positions, yet he was not always held in high regard by them. Crucial to his relationship with them was the oath of allegiance.

The Oath of Allegiance
The Germanic peoples did not distinguish between private and public law. They also did not grant institutions legal personality. The term *state* did not occur in Germanic law books. Only actual people had the right to enforce, rule, and possess. Frankish lords were not subordinate to the empire or the state, but to the individual person of the king. Their relationships to people in authority were personal. Frankish mayors and the royal descendants alike required political structure in these personal relations.

The oath of allegiance provided that structure. It is rooted in the concept of the *comitatus* (companionship), described by Tacitus in his *De Germania (On Germany)*, a treatise on the Germanic peoples. The

Carolingian miniature from the ninth century depicting animals in an idyllic garden

1171

Germanic leader had a group of crack troops called his "companionship," whose members had sworn their allegiance to the death. The leader would appear on the battlefield surrounded by these troops who deemed it the greatest honor to die for him.

Chalice with an image of Christ, commissioned on the occasion of his marriage by Tassilo of Bavaria, a Carolingian nobleman. The patron's name can be read on the bottom edge.

The concept appeared in several societies. Its traditions and values were deeply ingrained in Frankish society. The Merovingian kings had a form of comitatus. At their court, a *trustis* (trust) of warriors protected the king's person and property. The members of the trustis, the *antrustions,* were bound to their lord by oath. Various institutions in the Roman Empire were apparently comparable to the

Chanson de Roland (Song of Roland)

The only historical reference to the legendary hero Roland is a note by the Frankish scholar Einhard, contemporary biographer of Charlemagne. It gives Roland's Frankish name as Hruodlandus and states that he was warden on the borders of Brittany who died in battle in the Pyrenees. The oldest description of Roland's tragic fate is the French *Chanson de Roland*, which is thought to have been written in the late eleventh century. In the Middle Ages, there were many similar songs written by minstrels who traveled to the castles of the nobility and entertained the lords with tales of battle, love, loyalty, and bravery. There are many songs of Roland in European literature, all of which go back to the French original, although none excel it.

According to tradition, Roland was the nephew of Charlemagne and possessed the sword Durandel and the ivory horn Oliphant (Elephant). He accompanied Charlemagne on his military expedition against the Muslims in Spain in 778. As the army marched homeward over the Pyrenees, in the narrow Roncesvalles Pass high up in the mountains, it was forced to stretch out into a long line. The vanguard got farther and farther ahead of the soldiers in the rear. Charlemagne had ordered Roland to blow his horn, called Elephant, in case of emergency so the rest of the army could come to the rescue. The rear guard walked into an (Basque, according to Einhard) ambush. Not wanting to delay his king or put him in danger, Roland did not raise the alarm. Only when the entire rear guard was wiped out and Roland, badly wounded, remained alone, did he blow Elephant with his last ounce of strength. He smashed his famous sword to bits on the rocks so that it would not fall into enemy hands. Charlemagne rushed to the rescue only to find the lifeless body of his loyal vassal.

Two miniatures
from a fourteenth-century
manuscript depicting
the battle at Roncesvalles.
Above, the battle
is in full swing; below,
Charlemagne grieves
by the body of the fallen
Roland.

During Charlemagne's reign, Hārūn ar-Rashīd (known primarily from the *Tales of a Thousand and One Nights)* was the caliph of Baghdad. Trade between western Europe and the Islamic world increased as a result of their good relations. This cloth came from Iran to France in the eighth century.

Frankish comitatus. Landowners in Spain and Gaul had groups of warriors who were bound to their lord, but perhaps not by concepts of honor and trust. The lord offered protection as a patron. He provided modest remuneration and the warriors provided services in return.

Under the Germanic kings, institutions resembling the comitatus merged with those of the Roman estates. Over the course of time, a whole subservient class of *vassi* (vassals) emerged. The relationship was one of mutual obligation. The lord provided protection and maintained his vassal, who supplied services. It was a contract between unequals, giving both parties rights and obligations. Essential to it was the vassal's oath of allegiance to his lord.

Similar to this was the relationship that developed in Germanic society between the lord who paid his subordinates with landownership, or perhaps only with the right to farm a plot of land. The king did the same with his local administrators for the same reason: the use of money had disappeared. Remuneration could only be given in land.

The Fief

The development of the fiefdom was a central element in the development of the feudal system. Another important factor in allegiance, it had a larger political side, as well. As has already been emphasized, landownership was the basis of social position. Large landowners comprised an elite aristocracy expanded by the Carolingians through the large-scale granting of land in fief. Bishops and monasteries had been forced to hand over extensive holdings to the officers of newly formed cavalries. This at once weakened the power of the church and systematically linked personal loyalty to the transfer of land. The new aristocrats were bound by an oath of allegiance to the Carolingians and were not, therefore, as independent as the traditional landlords of the empire. Ultimately, this practice was to benefit Charlemagne.

However, the loyalty generated by the creation of fiefdoms depended in large part on the repeated conquests made by the king. New territories offered the promise of new landholdings for individual lords. This promise was already fading by the time Charlemagne was made emperor in 800. He had expanded his empire as far as he could. The nobility within his domain would have to live off their present estates.

By the turn of the century, Charlemagne not only lacked the resources for further foreign conquest, he had failed to develop the infrastructure to maintain what he had conquered. Innovative as he was in his efforts to educate the public and to bring about a cultural renaissance, he still had no money economy, which might have kept his lords content, no network of roads across his vast empire, no system of communication, and above all, no standing army or navy to protect his borders. The Vikings were already menacing the coasts.

A traditional German warrior with a lifetime of experience in war, Charlemagne was faced with a new challenge, the need to create a way to run his empire. He had to form a system of internal administration.

Internal Government
The empire was divided administratively into a large number of local districts, each called a *pagus* or *gau*. The local governor was called *comes* or *count* by the Franks. The number of gaus increased considerably as a result of Charlemagne's conquests, reaching well over two hundred. In a time when communication between regions was extremely limited and administrators were generally illiterate, any central governmental administration was practically impossible. The counts ran their gaus quite independently. Charlemagne looked for a way to preserve his central power within these limitations.

He appointed counts on a large scale, especially in the conquered territories of the Saxons and Lombards. He used trusted subordinates, aristocrats, and vassals for this, requiring them to swear the same oath of allegiance as was required for the fiefdom in order to obtain their positions. He soon required sitting counts to swear allegiance, as well, making the institution of the vassi into an instrument for exercising administrative power. Aristocrats had to reaffirm their subordination to the king in order to be allowed to rule small provinces.

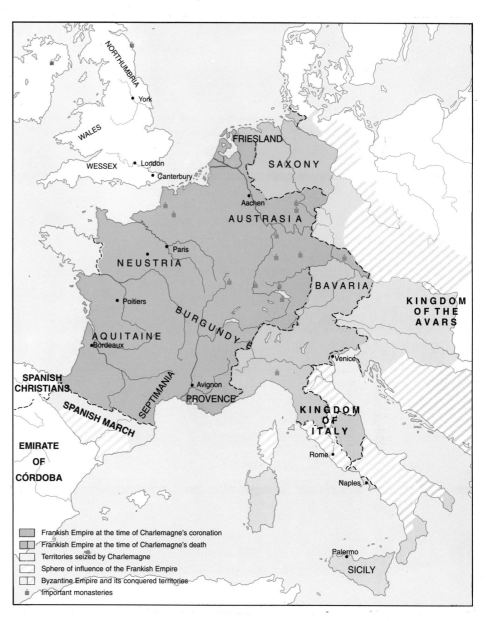

The typical components of the feudal system that would characterize political organization for centuries developed this way. The personal relationship (between lord and vassal) and the business relationship (between protector and liege man) were expressed in large landownership or administrative positions.

Charlemagne kept a tight rein on his counts, requiring administrative reports from them. He traveled extensively throughout the empire himself and sent out

The Carolingian Empire at the time of Charlemagne

Some of these were explicit instructions to administrative functionaries, some were detailed regulations, some punitive decrees, and others were imperial decrees of great importance. Among the capitularies found are orders to take the oath of allegiance, to teach all Christians to say the Lord's Prayer, and to organize a monastery properly. Charlemagne respected and recorded the traditions of many of the tribal peoples in his empire. Some of his most important capitularies served as addenda to tribal regulations.

Given the limited means available, Charlemagne's method created a certain guarantee of proper government in the extensive empire. Regional diversity, regardless of imperial attitude toward it, was a problem that could not be brought under control quite so easily. The empire was not a unit but a hodgepodge of core and conquered territories peopled by a mixture of tribes: Frisians, Lombards, Franks, Saxons, and others. The only way to unify it seemed to be to give the empire a dominant primary culture: an *Imperium Christianum,* an empire of Christians.

Gilded silver reliquary, inlaid with glass, semiprecious stones, and (Roman) cameos, in which the crown of Charlemagne's skull is kept

special trusted envoys called *missi dominici* (messengers of the lord, or royal messengers) to observe the gaus and maintain administrative contact with his court. Every count could expect surprise visits from the missi (usually a pair: a clerical official and a civil servant). The people of the gau were given a right of appeal to the missi. The emperor did not hesitate to depose any count guilty of bad administration in the eyes of the missi.

Imperial orders (called *capitularies)* originally oral, were recorded in writing toward the end of Charlemagne's reign.

The Western Empire

Christendom as a Rule

Few Carolingians remained content with military glory alone. In the eighth and ninth centuries, they conquered an enormous area. They needed to consolidate it, to combine the varied peoples they dominated not just under a single government but into a unified culture. The result would come to be called the Holy Roman Empire. Charlemagne, especially, recognized that an empire could not be maintained by the sword alone but required a stable economy and an active culture that could transcend

1177

Miniature from the Carolingian era showing church father St. Jerome surrounded by his pupils. It gives an indication of what clothing was like in the time of Charlemagne.

the ethnic diversity of a largely tribal realm. By the time of his coronation in 800, he had added Spanish March, Saxony, Bavaria, Carinthia, Lombardy, the Papal States, and Spoleto to his realm. Most of his people, including the aristocracy, were illiterate. Over the turbulent centuries since the fall of Rome, any remnants of interest in culture and scholarship outside the church had disappeared. Entire libraries had been lost. Education, always poor in terms of distribution and scale, had retreated behind the walls of monasteries. The extent of the decline is apparent from the sources we still possess. The few documents from the Merovingian era, phrased in abominable Latin, were written in barely legible scrawl.

Carolingian Renaissance

The first efforts at remedying the situation were made by Charles Martel, grandfather of Charlemagne. He imported scholarly English monks who must have been shocked at the literary situation on the continent. Their task was to educate a cadre of people to staff the court chancellery and to conduct diplomatic missions. The circumstances under which they began this first mission were favorable. Frankish rule had ensured a relatively high degree of safety throughout the empire.

Under Charlemagne, the same regime that had sent so many Saxons needlessly to their deaths offered protection to scholars and educators. The policies of baptism by the sword and capital punishment for rebellion now yielded place to new ones

advancing education, art, and culture. Charlemagne brought in intellectuals from his own empire and abroad to enlighten his court. He required his family and the laypeople of his entourage to study language, history, and theology. He added Latin and Greek to his native Old High German and (presumed) Frankish idiom. He even studied astronomy and mathematics. He established a library at the court and stocked it with works of theology and literature. He made the social life of his court an intellectual and cultural model for his empire.

Charlemagne carried his educational and cultural reforms first to the clergy and then to the entire population in what is called the Carolingian renaissance or rebirth. ("Rebirth" because the artists of the era consciously sought to emulate the achievements of the ancient Romans.) For centuries, most laypeople had shown no interest in education. Even the kings never learned to write, seeing little use for it. The few Franks needing matters recorded could employ a secretary, a *clericus* (clerk). The first Merovingians had secretaries who were laypeople, but generally anyone outside the clergy was illiterate.

This renaissance movement would escape its dependence on foreign experts in the course of time, but a key figure in the early effort was a well-read Anglo-Saxon monk, Alcuin. Charlemagne had invited him to reorganize education. Schools at the time were linked to monasteries and devoted exclusively to training for the priesthood. The curriculum was limited to reading and writing, some Latin

and psalm singing. While enough to enable the graduating priest to celebrate mass without mishap, it provided little of practical use. The consequences were apparent at the chancellery, the core of governmental administration. Surviving documents offer lasting proof of the substandard education of the staff employed there.

Alcuin established a palace school for imperial knights and a model school in Tours, where he became bishop and abbot at the same time. Alcuin put great emphasis on the study of Latin, no longer a living language. He explained in his famous *Epistula de litteris colendis* ("Letter on the necessity of learning letters"), written under Charlemagne's name, that it was essential to discuss the right faith (Christianity) in the right language to avoid misunderstanding. He was not opposed to the church schools, but to the content of their curriculum, which he changed, adding an Anglo-Saxon format. He used them to broaden the education of the clergy, and through it, to improve the level of popular education.

The Seven Liberal Arts
The seven liberal arts, once approved for Roman students, had been taught in England for two centuries. Alcuin reintroduced *musica, astronomia, geometria, dialectica, arithmetica, grammatica,* and *rhetorica* (music, astronomy, geometry, logic, arithmetic, grammar, and rhetoric) into the empire. This was a great deal more than psalm lyrics at the parish school. Those who completed Alcuin's course of

instruction could call themselves experts in every area covered by Western scholarship.

The liberal arts also provided an excellent basis for the schooling of clergymen: music was useful during the holy mass, astronomy enabled them to calculate the date of Easter, logic provided insight into theological problems, rhetoric and dialectics were useful at church synods, as grammar was in the library. Arithmetic and geometry were basic to economic matters and building.

Manuscripts
The study of the liberal arts meant the study of the classics. Alcuin made sure that manuscripts were available, literally handwriting or copying them in Latin with the help of scholars he trained. (The printing press would not be invented for centuries.) In a century without dictionaries, they produced a series of works that bore witness to an enormous vocabulary and high standard of grammar. His pupils acquired a surprising knowledge of the long-lost language, frequently even showing an ability to play with it. They saw themselves as picking up where the great classical

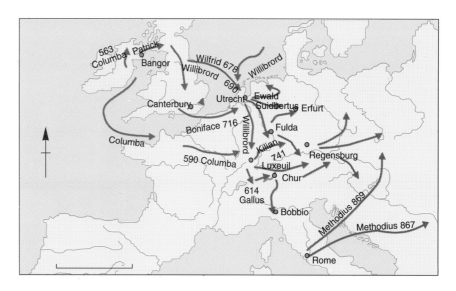

authors, Livy, Suetonius, and Virgil, had left off. The restoration had been achieved. Outside the school at Tours, other learned men helped Alcuin with his work. From Italy came Paulus Diaconus, who left behind a highly readable history of the Lombards, and from Spain, the Visigoth Theodulf, some of whose poetry survives.

Alcuin and his disciples introduced a simplified and legible script in their manuscripts that could be learned and written with relative ease. Called the Carolingian minuscule, that script is the forerunner of our modern font lettering.

Between the sixth and eighth century, a wave of conversion swept across western and central Europe, set in motion by Irish monks. They founded monasteries on the European continent that served as bases for their missionary journeys. The map shows the years of such journeys and the routes taken by a number of famous missionaries.

The missionaries frequently encountered strong popular opposition. Many died in the performance of their duties. One such priest was Boniface, murdered by the Frisians in 754 for chopping down an oak tree they considered sacred. Nevertheless, the persistence of the missionaries resulted in the conversion of most of Western Europe to Christianity after the year 1000. Modern statue of Boniface in Dokkum, the Netherlands

Charlemagne supported Alcuin and his colleagues wherever possible. He enjoyed conversing with the circle of learned men at his court. The high-ranking former illiterate seems to have felt at home in their company. He had clear and well-argued views on the major philosophical points of contention of his time. One of these was iconoclasm, an issue that rocked the Byzantine Empire in the eighth and ninth centuries.

The word, coming from the Greek *eikon* (image) and *kloein* (break), means the denouncing of the use of icons. In 726 and again in 730, Byzantine Emperor Leo III forbid the veneration of holy icons or images, in a decree condemned by the pope in Rome. Leo's son Constantine V, who succeeded him, went even further in 754, having their use condemned as idolatry by a church council at Hiera. Then the policy changed in Constantinople. Empress Irene, acting as regent for her son Constantine VI (whom she later imprisoned and blinded), summoned the second Council of Nicaea in 787 with the intent to restore the use of religious images. She succeeded; the council countenanced the practice and condemned the iconoclasts.

Charlemagne (or those writing for him) addressed the subject about 791 in the *Libri Carolini (Caroline Books)*. The work objects to the 787 decision at Nicaea by both Greek and papal authorities to approve veneration of icons, yet at the same time rebukes the iconoclasts for faithlessness. (Iconoclasm would come back in vogue once again in the East in the ninth century, only to be finally condemned in 843 at the Council of Orthodoxy.)

Frankish Scholars

"My life is a daily struggle against churlishness," complained Alcuin. While perhaps an exaggeration, it nevertheless expressed the way that he and his fellow scholars perceived themselves, as if they

Canon page from the so-called *Harley Gospels,* a Carolingian manuscript written in c. 800

CANON PRIMVS IN QVO QVATTVOR

MATTHEVS	MARCVS	LVCAS	IOHANNIS
VIII	III	VII	X
XI	IIII	X	VI
XI	IIII	X	XII
XI	IIII	X	XIII
XI	IIII	X	XXVIII
XIIII	V	XIII	XV
XXIII	XXVII	XVII	XLVI
XXIII	XXVII	XXXIIII	XLVI
XXIII	XXVII	XLV	XLVI
LXX	XX	XXXVII	XXXVIII
XCVIII	XCVI	CXVI	CXX
XCVIII	XCVI	CXVI	CXI
XCVIII	XCVI	CXVI	XL
XCVIII	XCVI	CXVI	CXLIII
XCVIII	XCVI	CXVI	CXXXVIII
XCVIII	XCVI	CXVI	CXXXI
CXXXII	XXXVII	LXXVII	CVIII
CXLI	LI	XVIII	LVIII
CXLII	LII	XXI	XXXV
CXLVII	LXIIII	XCIII	XLVII
CLXVI	LXXXII	XCIIII	LXXIII
CLXVI	LXXXII	XCIIII	XVII
CCVIII	CXVIII	CCXXXIIII	C
CCXI	CXXI	CCXXXVIII	XXXI
CCXX	CXXII	CCXXXVIII	LXXXV
CCXX	CXXVIII	CCXLII	LXXXVIII
CCXX	CXXVIII	CCLXI	LXXVI
CCXLIIII	CCXXVIII	CCL	CXLVI
CCXLIII	CCXXVIII	CCL	CXLI
CCLXIII	CLVI	CCLX	XX
CCLXXIII	CLVI	CCLX	XLVIII
CCLXXIII	CLVI	CCLX	XCVI
CCLXXVI	CLVIII	LXXXI	XCVIII
CCLXXX	CLXI	CCLXVIII	CXXII
CCLXXXIII	CLXV	CCLXVI	LV

1181

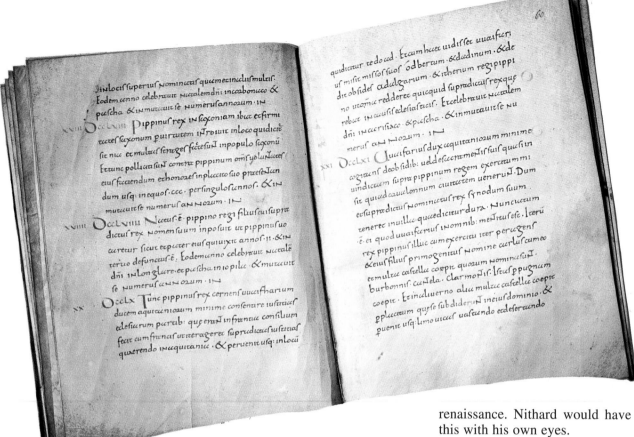

Two pages from the *Annalum Regium Francorum (Annals of the Franks)*, attributed to Einhard, which includes a description of the life of Charlemagne

were starting from nothing, faced with a barbarian horde to teach.

In fact, Alcuin had talented contemporaries among the Franks, most notably the monk Einhard, his former pupil. The young Frank had been sent to the palace school in 796. Befriended by Alcuin, he was also appointed superintendent of public buildings by Charlemagne. He acquired lasting reputation from the short biography of Charlemagne he wrote after the manner of Suetonius. That great Roman biographer saw history as a series of actions done by great men, a concept closely followed by Einhard. *The Life of Charlemagne,* more a study of the emperor's character than a work of any historical accuracy, is a prolonged work of praise. Einhard had great admiration for the emperor and was a major figure at his court. He was later to tutor the emperor's grandson Lothar I and be rewarded with large estates.

Einhard's fellow scholar Nithard managed to maintain greater distance from his subject in the history he wrote, but it is hardly uplifting. It is the story of the fratricidal struggle that ripped apart the Carolingian Empire and permanently destroyed the Carolingian dynasty and its renaissance. Nithard would have seen all this with his own eyes.

The Frankish authors did not restrict themselves to writing history. Something of the ferocity with which the Byzantine theologians of the era flew at each other drifted west. The better-educated priests within Charlemagne's empire conducted fierce debates, written and oral, among themselves. Some of the most polemical of them also wrote charming poetry.

Although it lasted but a generation after its founder, the Carolingian renaissance set the stage for medieval Europe. From a battered and disparate collection of peoples, it created a common culture within a single political and religious institution. Its dominant actor Charlemagne was seen as the model Christian emperor.

Cracks in the Empire

Charlemagne's last four years, according to his biographer Einhard, were marred by various fevers and ailments, including gout. He remarks that toward the end, the emperor dragged one leg. In 806, Charlemagne had prepared for his succession, planning to divide the empire among his three sons. By 813, the older two had died, eliminating any inheritance issues. The remaining son bore the same name as the great founder of the Frankish Empire: Ludwig. Louis, as he was called in the modified French version, had been king of Aquitaine since 781.

A year before his death, Charlemagne himself crowned Louis coemperor and designated him as sole successor. The pope was not invited to participate in this event because Charlemagne wanted to emphasize his own position. Although he had put his vast empire at the service of the church, he wanted to make the point that no one but God had more authority than he. He had insisted that the motto *imperator a deo coronatus* (emperor crowned by God) be included in his new laws for years. In fact, the right of the pope to crown the emperor would continue at least nominally for another 700 years.

"Emperor Charlemagne left this earth when he spent the winter at Aachen, more than 71 years old in the 47th year of his reign, the 43rd year since the conquest of Italy and the 14th since he had been declared Emperor and Augustus, on the 28th of January," recorded the imperial annuals. The year was 814.

Louis would have to prove himself to a power-hungry aristocracy, a domineering pope, and a multitude of foreign invaders. Above all else, he would have great difficulty in establishing a line of succession to follow him. He would not prove equal to these tasks. His self-assured style masked an indecisive man who found it difficult to take a stand and he let himself be easily used. Only his profound faith distinguished him at all, in the view of his court. This inspired his epithet, "the Pious."

Despite all the work of the Carolingians and the overriding power of Charlemagne at the top, the empire Louis inherited was anything but unified in the gaus. Each count already ran a virtually autonomous territory. Now the counts wanted to free themselves from imperial control. Not content with their separate spheres of influence, they wanted to make themselves masters of the lucrative royal rights across the land. The mintage of coins, the administration of justice, and the collection of tolls had been prerogatives of the king since the first Merovingians. Now they were being threatened by greedy subordinates.

Many of the counts tried to have their territories accorded the status of *immunitas* (immunity, a term in Roman law). During the late Principate, the imperial estates fell outside the powers of local civil servants and tax collectors. It was much more economical to administer them directly from the imperial palace. Illustratively enough, such imperial lands were referred to as "immunities." Being beyond local authority was generally beneficial to the landown-

ers. The practice was allowed to continue as the empire grew. Newly acquired regions were designated as immunities, added to the royal domains, and run the old way. The stewards representing the king on such estates found the situation attractive.

They rarely had to answer to the distant king and could not be touched by local concerns.

The term *immunity* gradually came to be used as a label for autonomy, desired by every landowner. Members of the Carolingian house, engaged in a fratricidal struggle for power, obliged, hurling titles, grants, and royal rights at the counts in

Carolingian ivory showing *(above)* the gospel story of the three women who discovered the empty tomb of Christ after his crucifixion. They are addressed by an angel. Below, the Roman soldiers guarding the tomb have fallen asleep. This panel has many similarities with Byzantine art of the same period. 1183

their efforts to win support. Many of the counts simply usurped the rights and vested them in a beleaguered Carolingian. They began to expand the scope of the concept of immunity, creating small states with their

Miniature from Lothar's evangelistary showing the Frankish king sitting on his throne

own administration of justice, coinage, and toll rights. This meant a massive loss of income to the imperial center, which weakened its power still further. The situation required a successful and charismatic leader like his father to hold the disconnected empire together. Louis was neither, unable even to hold his family together.

Fraternal Struggle

Almost at once, the question of who would succeed Louis presented itself. The emperor had three sons, Lothar I, Louis II (called Louis the German), and Pépin of Aquitaine. In 817, he made plans for their orderly succession, intending the eldest, Lothar, to get the title of emperor and his brothers to have subordinate kingdoms within the empire. He would subsequently add Charles II (Charles the Bald), his son by a second wife, at her insistence. His reign would be marked by division of the empire and rifts and reconciliations among the four brothers.

Louis's second wife favored her own son over her stepchildren and demanded that the emperor abide by the Salic law still in force that required division of the legacy between the sons. His outraged older sons rebelled against him in 830 and 833 and battled each other incessantly. The emperor himself seemed hardly concerned with the fuss. He never appeared to know exactly what was happening and, on several occasions, was no more than the prisoner of a temporarily victorious son. The death of Pépin in 838 made the battlefield a little clearer.

Lothar, as the eldest son, was entitled to the one thing that could not be divided, the emperor's crown. He therefore insisted on the unity of the empire. Charles and Louis were prepared to recognize his sovereignty for the sake of appearances, but no more than that. Lothar was crowned emperor by the pope in Rome in 840.

Six years earlier, the pious Louis, unwilling to continue his father's separate-from-Rome politics, had gone to Rome himself to be crowned again by the pope with much pomp and ceremony. Exactly what Charlemagne had feared had come to pass. The emperor had openly admitted that only a pope could crown him.

Lothar used all his talents, which lay primarily in the area of intrigue, to substantiate his title, trying to play off Louis and Charles the Bald against each other. All three brothers tried to gain popular support through extensive gift-giving in the gaus. Only the counts profited from the fraternal conflict, their prestige and independence growing with their wallets.

The Norman Threat

While the brothers fought one another, the Vikings (*Normands* in French) were discovering the treasures of a disintegrating empire. The Normans, the collective English name for these marauders from the north, had been appearing on the Frankish

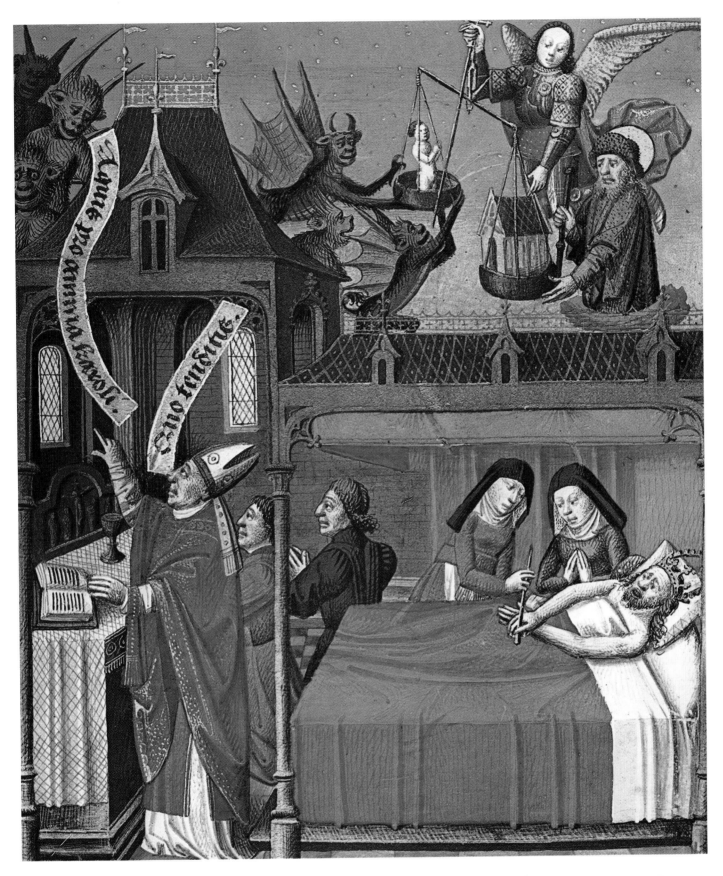

coasts for a century, initially as traders but later as raiders.

Their home territory was largely unknown to the people of western Europe outside of tales of a vast expanse of land, biting cold, and savage inhabitants. The people of Scandinavia, superb warriors, came from closely related clans of North Germanic origin. They still made use of the *comitatus*, with its concept of heroic valor, in their settlements. With almost no direct contact with the rest of Europe, they had heard virtually nothing about the Romans. They would not hear of

Fifteenth-century miniature depicting the death of Charlemagne in Aachen

The church of Reichenau, built over the ninth, tenth, and eleventh centuries, is typical of architecture from the Carolingian period.

A page from the Oath of Strasbourg sworn by Louis the German and Charles the Bald, against their brother Lothar I. The document is written in Carolingian minuscule, a script introduced by Alcuin that became the basis of all later European scripts.

Christianity until deep into the tenth century. For centuries, the Vikings had battled each other over territory, partly because of their customs of inheritance, totally different from those of the southern Franks. The oldest son received everything, the other children nothing. The younger ones simply claimed a new piece of land. After centuries, most of the land was taken. With too little land and agricultural techniques too primitive to feed a growing population, the Vikings faced a crisis. A class of landless warriors emerged with nowhere to go. At the same time, powerful chieftains began to create monarchies for themselves, early versions of modern Denmark, Sweden, and Norway. Under their rule, plundering was applauded, but not within the realm of the king. The landless had to go farther from home. The more enterprising of them took to the sea in search of trade and booty.

Charlemagne, recognizing the threat at least in part, had stationed fleets on the coasts of his empire for protection. His grandsons took no notice of the danger. The Normans used the rivers to pillage even inside the empire: the Seine to reach Rouen and even Paris for the first time in 845; the Loire for Nantes, Tours, Blois, Orléans, Bordeaux, and Angers in the decade after 863; the Somme for Amiens, Cambrai, Reims, and Soissons. They destroyed much of the Seine Valley over four years (856-860) but would form a permanent settlement there in 896. They gained a reputation for invincibility. No Carolingian dared to take serious action against them. By the end of the ninth century, individual counts gained immense prestige by organizing resistance to the Normans in their own regions. Men like Baldwin with the Iron Arm, who effectively defended Flanders over his whole lifetime, and Robert the Bold, a wealthy landowner who protected the Seine Valley, would prove with every victory that imperial power was useless and that only the local counts could guarantee security.

Regional commanders, often major landowners, were increasingly authorized by the kings to provide local defense. They regarded the areas they controlled as their own, to the point of making their titles to them hereditary. These domains formed the basis of a society increasingly feudal in nature.

Division of the Empire

The conflict between the brothers came to a head in 840 with the death of Louis the Pious. Lothar, who had been crowned by the pope, was recognized as emperor over the entire empire, backed by the church and the gau counts. They wanted to see a distant Lothar rather than a nearby Charles or Louis. The younger brothers had already laid the basis for their monarchies. Charles tried to rule in Gaul, Louis had greater success in the area around the Rhine. Lothar began to threaten their autonomy, only succeeding in uniting them against him. Together they defeated Lothar's troops in the bloody battle of Fontenay. The following year they ratified their alliance with the Oath of Strasbourg. Lothar was now ready to negotiate.

Treaty of Verdun: 843

The three brothers met in 843 at Verdun to divide their legacy. The disintegration of the empire was made official by the treaty they signed there. The borders were drawn to divide the imperial domains fairly. Louis II (also called Louis the German) received what had been the East Frankish kingdom and Charles, the West. These would become modern Germany and France, respectively. Lothar was given the imperial title and a central strip of land stretching from Friesland down to and including Rome, parts of Italy, the Lowlands, Alsace, Lorraine, and Burgundy.

Lothar's empire did not last long. It was divided among his children after his death, so that a row of weak buffer states emerged between Charles the Bald and Louis. In 870, the two kings divided the northern part of Lothar's legacy after the death of his oldest son, who had ruled it. The rest of the former emperor's domain fell into the

hands of a series of adventurers. His crown was claimed by various kings.

While the kings fought over the empty title to its throne, the empire disintegrated into hundreds of small states in the hands of the magnates. Charles the Bald had to defend his western realm against both the invading Vikings and his brother Louis the German. His decision to engage his powerful magnates in that defense, allotting them huge land tracts to command, established the subsequent feudal territories of France.

Charles the Bald, surrounded by courtiers, receives a Bible made for him by monks of the monastery at Tours. Ninth-century miniature

Heading off to Italy in 877, he promised the lords no one would tamper with those arrangements. This promise, in the 877 capitulary of Quierzy-sur-Oise, was regarded as an absolute principle by them after his death in October that same year.

Viking stele from Gotland, c. AD 700. The stone contains runic characters and an image of a Viking entering Valhalla, the hereafter, on an eight-legged horse.

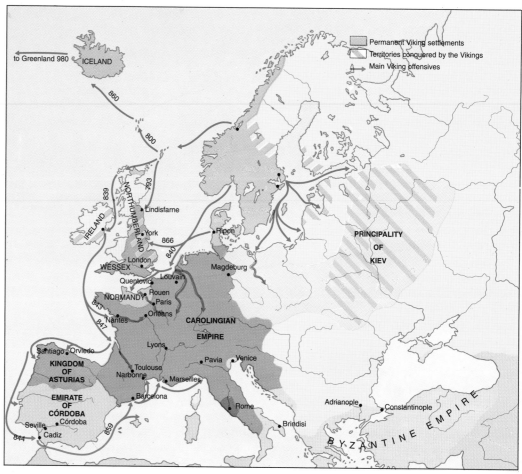

Viking expansion into western Europe in the ninth and tenth centuries

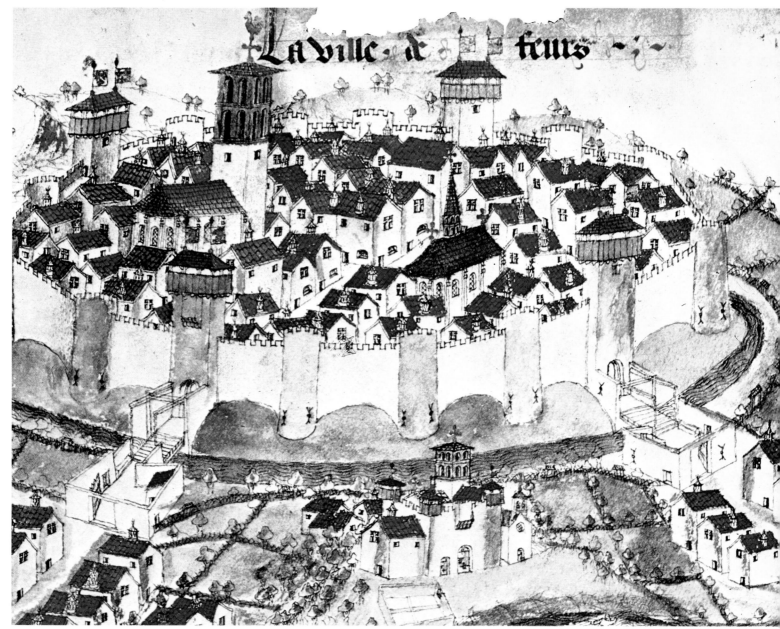

A medieval miniature showing the small walled city of Feurs on the river Loire in France. The drawbridges and the wide moat surrounding the walls made it possible to turn the city into an impregnable fortress during wartime.

Feudalism

A System of Lords and Serfs

By the time Charles the Bald died in 877, what remained of Charlemagne's system was chaos. The united Christian empire of which he had dreamed had degenerated into a multitude of autonomous and usually hereditary domains. Rather than unified by a common culture, the society had become a seething mass of vying kings and counts, priests, popes, and plunderers. The political, economic, and social system called feudalism, already evolving, emerged out of the chaos.

Feudalism
The precise origin of the word *feudalism* is unclear. It appears to derive from the

Middle English *feo* (cattle), the Anglo-Saxon *feoh* (cattle) plus *od* (wealth), and the Latin *feodum* or *feudum* (literally meaning cattle-wealth). In Middle English, *feo* or *fee* meant fief or payment, the land from a feudal lord held by a lesser one in return for services.

Land, worked by serfs, was held by vassals in return for the military services and the fealty they pledged to the actual landowner. Vassalage itself was an obligation owed to the overlord in return for the right to a fief. The overlords, the great landowners, in turn, bound themselves to the king. As their wealth and power increased, that of the king diminished.

The oath of allegiance to the king required in Charlemagne's era became, within a generation, merely a formality

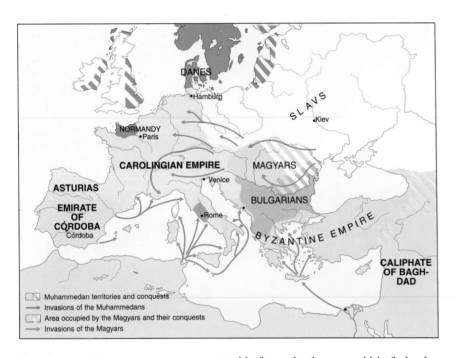

The advance of the Muslims and the Magyars into Western Europe in the ninth century

expected before a lord assumed his father's position. Central authority had lost all its effectiveness. The emperors had become the playthings of the quarreling territorial princes, brought to power at their whim. Kings, forced to buy the support of the nobility with their own crown domains, had little more than the palaces left to them by their forefathers. In the end, lacking any property of their own to use for influence, they were made and broken by the great landowners, the magnates. Some of this was beyond the control of any emperor; some of it was not.

Carolingian Succession
No Carolingian after the sons of Louis the Pious was capable of dealing with the problems of his realm. While the magnates were still expanding their autonomy and

amassing their prestige and wealth, Lothar, Louis II, and Charles battled each other. Yet each had the skills to govern. Their successors, with few exceptions, were incapable of making a decent decision. Contemporaries emphasized their feebleness with vicious epithets.

Louis the Stammerer, son and successor to Charles the Bald, died two years after his father, leaving the throne to his sons.

Both died by 884. Charles III the Fat, the only remaining son of Louis II the German and heir to the Eastern Frankish crown (of Germany), now took the Western crown from the baby Charles the Simple. It might have been better off with the baby. Charles the Fat was so incompetent he was deposed by the East Franks in less than four years.

That revolt was led by Arnulf, illegitimate son of the East Frankish ruler Carloman, who was a great-grandson of Charlemagne. Considered the only really energetic descendant of the Carolingians to ascend any throne, he repulsed the Vikings, who were invading his kingdom in 891. He campaigned in Italy in 894 and again in 895-896. In early 896, he captured Rome and was crowned Holy Roman emperor, the last Carolingian to be so invested. When he died in 899, jealous

The facade of the mosque (now also housing a cathedral) of Córdoba, the magnificent city of the Muslim caliphs in Spain

nobles put his son Louis the Child only on the East Frankish throne and not that of the Holy Roman Empire.

In 888, after the death of Charles the Fat (deposed only in the East), powerful magnates offered the West Frankish crown to Count Odo, or Eudes, son of Robert the Bold, the first Robertian to take it from the Carolingians. Opposing magnates crowned Charles the Simple in 893. Dynastic rivalry ensued until 987, when the Capetian heirs to the Robertians would end the Carolingian line.

There was a half-century Carolingian interlude. Eudes died in 898. His brother

Robert I, elected king in 922 by magnates opposing Charles the Simple, was killed in battle a year later. His son-in-law Rudolph took his place, imprisoning Charles (who died in prison in 929). Yet on the death of Rudolph in 936, his successor Hugh the Great, son of Robert I, stepped aside for Louis IV, son of Charles the Simple. He did much to restore past Carolingian glory, leaving a son and a grandson to reign, but the impoverished royal line could not prevail against the tide of social change.

Vandals

As the ninth and tenth centuries passed, Christian Europe fell into deep crisis, vandalized by all the other folk whom God, according to the ideas of the time, had sent to punish his people. Christianity came under attack on three fronts.

The Normans

The Vikings or Northmen, also called Normans, had been pillaging along the coasts and riverbanks for some centuries before Arnulf inflicted the resounding defeat on them in the East Frankish Empire in 891. They had a fearsome reputation. In Ireland, for example, they undertook the difficult and dangerous journey to the rocky island of Great Skellig, where a colony of hermit monks lived. When they found only the impoverished hermits and a few bare fields, they murdered the whole population in vengeance. The island has been deserted to this day.

The Normans had primarily targeted churches and monasteries. This was not

Upper section
of a decorated Norman
(Viking) scabbard

Tenth-century miniature that depicts a small ship. Because of Muslim territorial expansion and Norman invasions, the Christians had almost no power at sea.

1192

Alfred the Great (849-899)

Alfred, the youngest of five sons of King Aethelwulf, succeeded his brother Aethelred as king of the West Saxons (Wessex) in Great Britain in 871, in the midst of one of the frequent Danish incursions. He made peace with the Danes in 873, only to see it ignored five years later. He assembled an army at Athelney and used it to capture the main Danish stronghold. By 886, he had retaken London from the Danes and been recognized as king of all England. He had new weapons forged and a fleet of ships built. England was ready when the Danes invaded again in 893. Over the next four years of war, the Danes were driven out of the country.

Alfred also promoted education. Like Charlemagne, he built a court school where he had noted scholars teach, including the Welsh monk Asser and the Irish theologian John Scotus Erigena. He decreed that all free-born children in England were to learn to read and write. He set a good example by learning to do so himself and by mastering Latin at an advanced age. He is credited with translating a variety of works into Anglo-Saxon to foster popular solidarity, providing some with supplements. These include *The History against the Pagans* and *The History of the World* by the Spanish priest Paulus Orosius, written after the fall of Rome in 410 to comfort the believers; *Regula Pastoralis (Pastoral Care)* by Pope Gregory I, which he gave to the English bishops to serve as a guide; and *The Consolation of Philosophy* by the Roman philosopher Boethius.

He wrote the first new laws in over a century. Reflecting his interest in integrating his country, they did not distinguish between the English and the Welsh. Alfred created the basis for the unification of England.

The so-called Alfred Jewel from the ninth century, with a portrait of Alfred the Great. The inscription reads: "commissioned by Alfred."

anti-Christian zeal, but simple greed. That was where the greatest treasures were kept. They had managed to establish a settlement in the Seine Valley in 896, in part because the Carolingians' attitude toward them was ambivalent. Not only were the Normans related to the Franks, both part of the Germanic language group, they were quite prepared to embrace the Christian faith if it served them. In 911, Charles the Simple granted them the fertile area of the Lower Seine Valley that still bears their name, Normandy. The people who stabled their horses in the Carolingian chapel in Aachen would one day break the might of the Saracen robber bands on Sicily.

Magyars

Another people who had just reached the lowlands of the mid-Danube region, like the Normans, recognized the chances the chaotic realm offered. Ominously, they chose to settle at the same place where Attila ("the Scourge of God") had once set up his headquarters. The newcomers resembled his hordes in other respects, as well. Like them, these terrifying horsemen dared to range hundreds of miles in search of plunder. Called the Magyars (later, became the name Hungarians), they pillaged the interior of the Eastern Frankish Empire. They never reached the coasts, ravaged by Normans, nor had contact with the Arab marauders called Saracens.

Arabs

It was the heyday of the Arab states bordering the Mediterranean. The Shiites had established the splendid Muslim state (or caliphate) of the Fatimids in Cairo. Muslim fleets controlled the seas. "The Christians cannot float a plank on the Mediterranean," claimed an Islamic writer.

Muslim hordes invaded the land in search of plunder and slaves. The Christians hardly dared to defend themselves. In Italy, they built towers next to their churches in order to be able to spot the enemies in time to flee. The invasion went far beyond marauding expeditions.

Detail of a twelfth- or thirteenth-century miniature, showing mills powered by water. Such mills were used to irrigate the land and to grind grain.

Once, a Muslim fleet even occupied Ostia, the port city of Rome. The Muslims built permanent operating bases for themselves. They established an emirate on Sicily, turning Palermo into a city almost as brilliant as Cairo or Córdoba, Spain. They occupied a part of southern Italy and even succeeded in taking Fraxinetum in southern Gaul. In Córdoba, the Umayyad emirs became so powerful they could get away with giving themselves the title of caliph, secular and religious successors to Muhammad.

Freemen and Serfs

Faced with the collapse of imperial power and the threats of vandals on all sides, the position of the ordinary freemen in the Frankish Empire and its aftermath was hardly desirable. Freemen, mostly peasants with their own farms, formed a considerable grouping under Charlemagne. They formed no part of the economy of the great estates and were dependent for the protection of their property and person on the king. When Carolingian power disintegrated, they were completely unprotected.

In contrast to them, serfs had the right to protection, such as it was, traditionally given by their lords in return for labor. In the absence of any centralized army, only the military potential of individual estates

Section of a twelfth-century pier capital originating from Burgundy, which shows a farmer about to empty a basket of grapes into a winepress.

Twelfth-century chess pieces made of walrus ivory. They were found on the Orkney Islands in the north of Great Britain, and show influence of Viking artistic traditions, particularly the winged dragons and interlace ornament on the backs of the pieces.

kept plunderers at bay. Feudal lords developed the "castle" as part of their defense. The term is misleading; this construction holds no comparison to the impressive stone fortress built in later centuries. The early castle was little more than a strong drumlike tower of wood and loam with small openings for weaponry. Damp hides offered the only protection against hostile

Cover of Charles the Bald's Psalter. In the middle is an image carved in ivory and framed by jewels mounted in gold.

arsonists; besieged and besieger were frequently separated by only a wall of planks.

Ordinary freemen were not owed even this protection. The royal palace, far away and in dispute, could not help them. They had to give up their freedom to get onto an estate. A great mass of once independent farmers lost so much of their freedom they could be bought and sold, farms and all. By the tenth century, the class of free farmers had all but disappeared in some parts of Europe. The landowners had them all.

Once under landlord authority, free farmers, assuming their farms went with them, became serfs, little different than the hereditary tenant farmers already on the estate. Real slaves existed, too, but in small numbers because there was little worth doing with them. A human being alone had no value. Only the combination of farm and person was valuable. The few slaves a landlord owned generally performed only household tasks. Usually, the estate was divided into several domains, the main one of the lord and the smaller holdings of the tenant farmers who paid the lord shares of their crops, the first calf of the year, for example, or a percentage of the eggs. In some areas, a system of forced labor known as corvée came into existence. Tenants worked a number of days a week on the farmland the lord had reserved for himself. The extent and nature of labor varied considerably from region to region, but these obligations held the whole agricultural system together.

The peasants, whether free or serf, were seen as the bottom of society. The prevailing concept was of the universe as a pyramid with God at the top. Within that great whole, everyone had his fixed task and position. Three classes emerged: the peasants, the clergy, and the nobility. Each had its specific task, according to a Middle Dutch author: "The first bakes, the second prays, and the third wields the sword." These tasks were seen as assigned by God; it was regarded as a sin to leave one's place.

Lords and Rulers

The changing nature of imperial power and its confrontation with an increasingly dominant aristocracy is best illustrated with a couple of anecdotes: the rise of Count Baldwin and the fall of King Zwentibold.

No one knows who Baldwin was. Some maintain he was a parvenu, an upstart new to wealth and power; others insist he was descended from an ancient aristocratic family. At any rate, he ran a few *gaus* (districts) in the marshy delta around the river Scheldt. One of them, Flanders, contained the city of Bruges. Baldwin was a well-known figure at the court of Charles the Bald, king of the Western Frankish Empire. Princess Judith fell passionately in love with him. The affection was mutual. Charles the Bald forbade his daughter to see Baldwin, and just to be on the safe side, shut her up in the Senlis palace. Baldwin did not forget his love. With the knowledge of her brother Louis, he planned her abduction. Judith went with her count to Flanders and married him.

Charles the Bald was beside himself with rage. He could do nothing. Given the resources he had available, he could not even consider going to war. His only recourse at the time was diplomacy. He managed to get Pope Nicholas to declare the marriage annulled. This set the church against Baldwin. The bishops of both the Rhine and the Meuse regions began to isolate him from his peers. Baldwin was not impressed. He let it be known that he was considering an alliance with the Normans. This was blatant blackmail, but it worked. Even Pope Nicholas, who was not easily alarmed, changed his mind. He told Charles that he feared "that your rage and

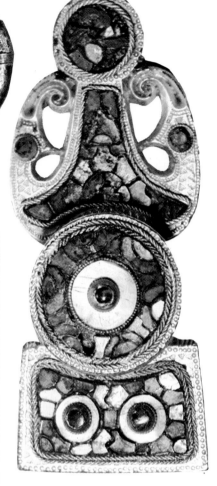

Bronze fibulas (pins), decorated with gold and silver, made by Norman artists

Page from a Greek manuscript, showing the construction of a church in the margin

indignation will cause Baldwin to bind himself to the godless Normans, the enemies of the Holy Church." Charles the Bald was forced to recognize the marriage. He restored Baldwin to favor and greatly increased his holdings.

The resolute count went down in history as Baldwin with the Iron Arm, a well-deserved epithet. Not only a famous lover, Baldwin also managed to defend his lands

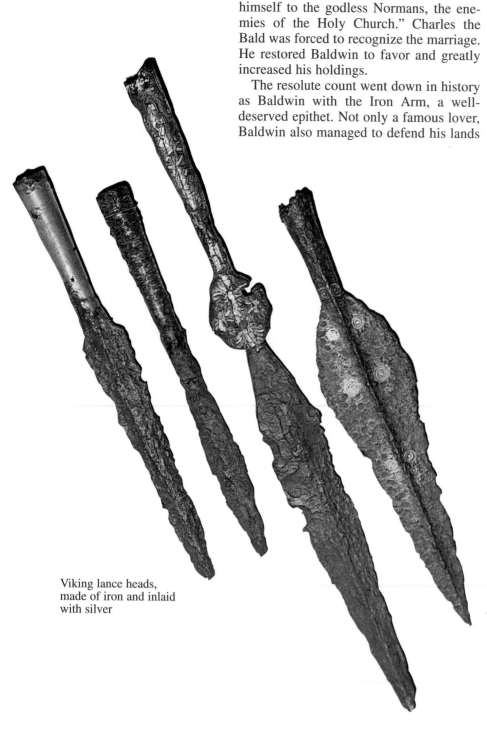

Viking lance heads, made of iron and inlaid with silver

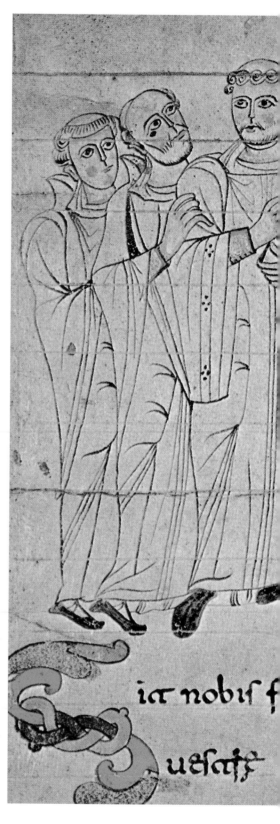

against all invaders. Even in a time when Norman violence was everywhere, the Scandinavian marauders generally stayed out of his territory. Once they chanced a landing, but the Flemish farmers, led by Baldwin, drove them back to their ships.

Baldwin's progeny displayed the same prowess as their forefather. They expanded their territory, established their independence from the king, and defended their country against invaders. They also succeeded in taking charge of the royal domains within their territory, increasing their own power and curtailing that of the

king. They usurped the royal prerogatives of fine, toll collection, and judgment, assuring themselves of great power and important income. Baldwin with the Iron Arm became the founder of a dynasty of powerful counts, whose regional territory called Flanders, emerging in the first quarter of the tenth century, was to remain a political unit for centuries. The Flanders model of a nobility takeover of

imperial authority, with or without the associated romance, was very common in the Frankish Empire.

The story of the Carolingian Zwentibold illustrates the point from the imperial perspective. King of a heathland near Susteren and illegitimate son of Arnulf of Carinthia, Zwentibold suffered an experience the opposite of Baldwin. Arnulf, himself an illegitimate grandson of Louis the German,

had defeated the Normans at the Dijle and conducted victorious campaigns against various Slavic tribes in the east. Arnulf now wanted to restore Carolingian power in Lotharingia. Over the years, local nobles in that region (part of the legacy of Lothar deeded to Louis the German by the Treaty of Meerssen) had made themselves virtually independent. Arnulf persuaded them to accept his son Zwentibold as king. The

Monks are being ordained as priests by a bishop in this miniature from a tenth-century manuscript.

1199

nobles officially agreed, paying homage to him in diet (formal assembly) but when Zwentibold attempted to depose a number of them to reinforce his control, they openly rebelled. Lacking any means of enforcement, he yielded the field to the nobles. He died in 900 near Susteren, surrounded by a few faithful followers. His fate was typical of Carolingians confronted by the rising nobility: royalty had no real basis of power left. The nobles simply sold their support to the highest bidder.

The Clergy

Despite the change in the relative positions of royalty and nobility, the social position of the church remained unshaken. Both peasant class and nobility looked to it, expecting the priests to ward off evil spir-

Serfs harvesting and pressing grapes in the presence of their master

its, some possibly of political origin. The bishops exerted great political influence. A man like Hincmar, bishop of Reims, was not to be treated lightly. His coercive letters on matters he considered important often achieved much more than armed force. Pope Nicholas treated the Frankish kings and the other powerful men of his time as if they were his own acolytes, servants at his personal altar. Seen by the faithful as personifying the church, he claimed to exert authority over people's souls and their political lives.

In addition to the significant influence it wielded through its spiritual authority and that of its noted personages, the church still retained enormous power because the church still held considerable land. This was true despite the dispossession efforts of Charles Martel in his attempt to fund a cavalry in the previous century. The bequests of repentant sinners, certainly

encouraged by the priests, increased church property holdings still further.

Another major factor in its importance was the church's control over the highly prized right to accession, to a bishop's see, for example, or to an appointment as abbot. It was customary for nobles to try to help their relatives attain such positions for entirely mundane reasons: to give them a permanent roof over their heads and a means of support for their families. Religious and worldly lords came from the same families and frequently represented the same interests. The stringent requirements of the Christian priesthood, such as celibacy, often held in little regard, were considered of secondary importance. The phenomenon of piety would only gain importance in the eleventh and twelfth centuries. The hierarchy of the church entered the nobility's sphere of interest.

The clergy of the lower orders, the pastoral or local monks, were required to be obedient. Expected to maintain the monastery to which they were assigned and to speak Latin, a language strange to them, they were generally better educated but just as poor as the peasants. The common opinion was that if they did receive small tokens of appreciation from the flock, it did no harm.

Taken as a whole, the clergy was considered a separate social entity, as distinct from nobility and peasantry, but, in practice, its social composition was the same. It drew its members from the population around it and its hierarchy reflected that of the larger society. The lower orders of the church were comprised of ordinary peasants, while the higher levels (prelates and above) were of noble birth. The church was a mighty institution in a feudal society that had developed over centuries. Its rulers had a stake in maintaining the status quo. They made feudal ideology a part of Christianity, justifying, approving, and sanctifying the system of feudalism. The network of mutual obligations begun as response to economic forces took on political importance, was made social tradition, and finally acquired divine color through the involvement of the church. The social contract was regarded as the will of God.

Feudal society was static, holding its members prisoner in specific tasks, its arrangements blessed by the church. There was no place in it for anyone who did not behave according to its demands. Escape would come in urban form. In the cities, soon to be established by the thousands all over Europe, a completely different type of society would develop.

Tenth-century miniature depicting the palace of Otto I. The king is receiving a delegation. His wife is next to him. On the left, a group of courtiers is listening to the discussion.

The Feudal Society

The Structure of the Empire

The development of feudal society in Europe was a process lasting hundreds of years, from the early tenth through the thirteenth century. A social phenomenon, feudalism grew out of and then reinforced the economic and political conditions of the continent. It took on different aspects in various places, but had certain core characteristics, most notably the defining of people in relation to the land. Owned by overlords, land, worked by serfs attached to it, was given in fief or put under the management of vassals in exchange for military and other services. This arrangement of

1201

interlocking social contracts had major impact on the lives of most individuals of the era, restricting them to the class and function by which they were categorized. The system was static, sanctioned by the major religious institution of Europe, the Christian church, which disapproved of attempts at social change or individual mobility. The feudal universe was commonly viewed as a pyramid with God at the top and nobles, clergy, and peasants arranged in descending order. The place of the king in that picture was not clear as the tenth century began.

The Eastern Frankish Region

Although much of the Eastern Frankish Empire had only briefly experienced unification under the Carolingian dynasty, it was far less fragmented than its neighboring western counterpart, and far less feudal in nature. Many of the factors contributing to the development of feudalism had never existed in the east. Old tribal traditions, cultures, and loyalties still dominated there. The region was made up of five large dukedoms, four of which were based on tribes: the Saxons, the Franks, the Swabians, and the Bavarians. The fifth dukedom, Lotharingia, was a rather loosely organized region that had no relationship to a pre-Carolingian tribe. Power in each region was concentrated in the hands of its duke.

Louis the Child (893-911)

The sickly Louis the Child, the son of Arnulf, was born in 893 and made king of the German empire in 899. (Louis did not succeed his father as Holy Roman emperor. He died in 911, before reaching adulthood.) Hatto I, archbishop of Mainz, governed for him as regent. The kings by now had already lost any major role in administration. It was a time of frequent Hungarian invasions and limited governmental power. The eastern nobles took the opportunity to make themselves quite independent of any royal authority.

Conrad

After the death of Louis the Child, the regional dukes proclaimed a successor although they really had little use for a royal leader. Bypassing the Western Frankish king, Charles the Foolish (or Charles the Simple), they chose one of their own, Duke Conrad the Frank. He spent his reign fighting bands of Slavs and Magyars and his own feudal dukes. His attempt to elicit his electors' respect for the crown's authority failed. He died in 918, unable to establish a royal dynasty and, unlike the kings before him, never receiving the crown of Holy Roman emperor from the pope. One of his major opponents was Henry, Duke of Saxony. After Conrad's death, those of the nobility still prepared to go to the diet (only Franconian and Saxon nobles were) chose Henry as his successor in 919. The story goes that the duke heard of his appointment while hawking, hence his nickname: the Fowler. The dukes of Bavaria, Swabia, and Lotharingia refused to acknowledge him as king until 925. Called Henry I, he was the first in a Saxon line of German kings.

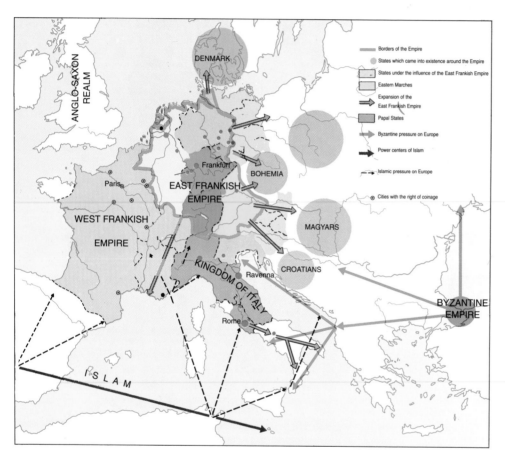

Europe at the time of the East Frankish Empire

Henry the Fowler (876?-939)

In the eyes of his electors, Henry the Fowler was an ideal king. He had learned from Conrad's mistake and made no attempt to rule his fractious nobility. He sought only nominal recognition as king, recognizing that he could have no real authority without the power to back it up. He occupied himself exclusively with his own duchy, Saxony, with great success.

In 919, he added significantly to his domain. He encouraged the emigration of his subjects to the Swabian regions in the east to expand his influence there. He fought and defeated the Magyars who, during Conrad's regime, had plundered the region as far as Burgundy and Lorraine. In 926, he arranged a nine-year truce with them, using the time to build up the defenses of Saxon villages, training troops of mounted warriors. So protected, many of the villages developed into cities.

The absentee king built up his regional power base without offending the Eastern

Eleventh-century miniature depicting serfs loyal to different lords fighting in a vineyard

1203

Miniature from
the time of Otto I showing
how the king is honored

Franks, successfully defending it against the Wends in 929, a Magyar invasion in Thuringia in 933, and the Danes in 934. He added the territory he seized from them to his own. By the time he died in 936, he had become the most powerful man in the empire and had created a united Germany. Never granted the imperial crown, he is nevertheless generally considered one of the Holy Roman emperors.

Otto the Great (912-973)

His son Otto was approved as king of Germany at once. The diet that was called to consider the appointment was almost a formality. The dukes were more than happy to pass on the crown to the son of the inordinately successful man who had let them alone so consistently.

Some of the dukes would live to rue their decision. At first, Otto pursued his father's policy of avoiding conflict with the nobles, but his brother persuaded some of them to revolt against him. The young king was forced to depose the rebellious dukes. He succeeded in forcing his subjects to accept some of his own faithful followers and relatives as replacement dukes.

Many of these, even his sons, turned out to be no more loyal to him than their predecessors. Otto looked around for other ways to establish his authority.

The Religious State System

The only powerful group in the Frankish Empire outside the rebellious nobility was the higher clergy, drawn from the same social stratum. Otto decided to make it dependent on him. He began to pay assiduous attention to church matters, establishing new bishoprics and granting bishops and abbots extensive lands in fief. He retained the predominant voice for himself and the right to determine who should be appointed as bishop-administrator. The church had traditionally supported the power of the crown. However, of greater importance to Otto was the fact that clerics were never allowed to legally marry. Any children they had (and they did have them) were by definition illegitimate, with no right of succession. Clerics, in other words, could never create a feudal dynasty; the king would always be returned what he had granted in fief. Ambitious prelates would only strengthen his authority.

The bishoprics Otto created and the accompanying lands he granted in fief became centers of royal authority, the first ones eligible for any additional fiefs that became vacant. In this area where the bishops already exercised full spiritual power, this political design, the religious state system, increasingly undermined the authority of the secular lords and reinforced Otto's position.

The biblical king David is shown playing his harp in this tenth-century miniature.

1205

Italy

Otto's court had been a refuge for Italian exiles for many years, and the king took great interest in what was happening on the other side of the Alps. Italy, originally part of Lothar's legacy, had been partitioned and given its own king. Since the death of the last Carolingian king and emperor, Louis the Blind, various pretenders had been fighting for the throne and control of the papacy, despite its limited power.

In 951, one of the most powerful pretenders died. Berengar II usurped his kingdom and prepared to marry his widow Adelaide, queen of Lombardy. Adelaide appealed to Otto for help. The king marched in with his army, liberated Adelaide, and married her himself, becom-

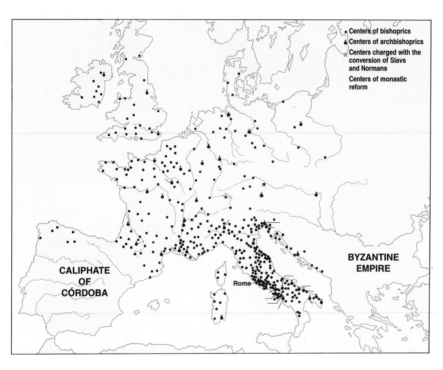

The Christian church in the West at the time of the East Frankish Empire

Centers of bishoprics
Centers of archbishoprics
Centers charged with the conversion of Slavs and Normans
Centers of monastic reform

CALIPHATE OF CÓRDOBA

Rome

BYZANTINE EMPIRE

ing ruler of northern Italy. Whether there was any romance in the union is not mentioned by any chronicler. There were other candidates for the hand of Adelaide, the king of Burgundy and Otto's own dukes among them. What counted was immediate action, which Otto provided.

The new throne made Otto the most powerful ruler in Europe. The emperorship would have served to confirm this fact, but he had to return north to put down yet another rebellion among his nobles, this time led by his son Liudolf. In 955, he stopped a Magyar invasion. At the battle of Lechfeld, he inflicted such losses on them they never tried again.

Otto's Coronation

Six years later, Otto intervened once more in Italy, where Berengar had managed to

The Normans and England

While Charlemagne reigned, England was not yet united. In Scandinavia, possibly due to a shortage of land and a need for new markets, Nordic people (collectively called Vikings, Northmen, or Normans) began expeditions along the coasts of Europe. Traveling by relatively small open boats (Viking ships), largely in ethnic groups, they raided, traded, and eventually settled areas of eastern Europe (primarily the Swedes), Greenland (the Norwegians), Germany, France, Spain, and England (the Danes and, less so, the Norwegians).

In 793, the first Norwegian marauders burned down the monastery on the Island of Lindisfarne, just northeast of England. England, divided into many kingdoms, was easy prey. Over the next two centuries, Danish invasions became a frequent occurrence. Only Alfred the Great (849-899), king of powerful Wessex in the south, was able to withstand the plunderers.

Aethelred the Unready, Anglo-Saxon king of England (978-1016), tried to fend off invasion by paying a huge annual tribute he raised by taxes called *Danegeld* (from *geld* or money). This was the first western system of direct taxation. Later, the Danegeld came to form the basis of the English royal treasury.

In the eleventh century, King Canute (Cnut) II briefly formed a North Sea empire that included England, Denmark, and Norway. Danes and Norwegians conquered northern England, eventually establishing the kingdom called the Danelaw, taking up farming and trading, and creating new commercial centers like York. They took over parts of Scotland, including its northern Isles and the Hebrides, and Ireland, founding the towns of Waterford, Wexford, Limerick, and Dublin. They left a lasting impact on forms of administration, language, and law.

regain his old position. Otto drove him out and this time was able to reach Rome. He was crowned Otto I, Holy Roman emperor, in 962. Pope John XII was a young man of twenty-six, much given to drinking, and the weak-willed puppet of a Roman faction. Otto deposed him in 963 and had Leo VIII elected in his place. The emperor controlled the bishop of Rome as he did his bishops at home.

This 66-foot (22-meters)-long Viking ship was found in a grave in Norway. The Normans used such ships to make their journeys to western and southern Europe.

A *fibula*, or clasp used to hold clothing together, made by the Normans from beaten metal

After Otto's coronation, only kings from the East Frankish region were crowned emperor. They based their claims to rule not only Italy but all Christians on Otto's accomplishments. His success, however, was mixed. Able to hold the empire together throughout his lifetime, he was unsuccessful in his attempts to gain a permanent foothold in Italy. Unable to negotiate an alliance between the Byzantine Empire

1207

Twelfth-century fresco depicting the mounted Pope Silvester making a ceremonial ride through the streets of Rome

and his own, he nevertheless did arrange a marriage between Theophano, daughter of the Byzantine emperor Romanus II, and his son Otto II. Seeking to make the church subordinate to his own authority, Otto the Great, as he is usually known, in fact fostered the spread of Christianity. Otto's coronation ceremony itself carried significance. John XII had an unpleasant surprise

in store for the new emperor. Along with his crown, he received a beautifully decorated copy of the Donation of Constantine, which must have been intended as a warning. Dating from the early days of the Rome-Byzantium split, this document, eventually proven a forgery, purported to prove that Constantine had given ("donated") the pope title to the West. John XII, in

giving the copy to Otto, was reminding him that the papacy still held absolute power over any monarch of the West.

The West Frankish Region
During the course of the tenth century, the West Frankish Empire was divided among a number of powerful nobles, any of whom could have defeated the king. Such men as the lords of Burgundy, the counts of Anjou, and the dukes of Normandy made the crown nothing more than an ornament. The kings retained virtually no genuine power.

The Capetians
In 987, on the death of Louis V, the last of the Carolingian kings of France, the combined forces of the nobility and the clergy gave the vacant throne to Hugh Capet, a descendant of Robert the Bold and of Odo. Although he was duke of France and count of Paris, Hugh was elected king actually because he lacked the influence to control the other magnates. He was only able to get them to elect him through a combination of armed might, church support (he was a dedicated member), and bribery, turning over title to some of his land to the electors. Capet's domain was a tiny bit of land between Paris and Orléans, a minute fraction of Charlemagne's legacy called Île-de-France, the area immediately around Paris. The nobles miscalculated the future. Capet would establish a dynasty of kings that would rule France for more than three centuries.

Significantly, soon after Hugh became king, he arranged to have his son Robert (called the Pious) crowned, appointing him as an associate to share the imperial reign. The move set precedent. When Robert assumed the throne (as Robert II) in 996, he named his own eldest son Hugh to succeed him. Capetian fathers would share at least partial rule with their eldest sons until the end of the twelfth century. When Hugh died, his brother Henry became king in 1031. The Capetians, claiming a principle of heredity, continued to hand down the crown through a direct male line until 1328. (Charles IV died that year with no male heirs. A related family, the Valois, would take over France for another two and a half centuries.)

The Capetians set other precedents that would enhance their power. Like his eastern counterpart Henry the Fowler, Hugh Capet understood the importance of not meddling in the politics of the powerful vassals. He and his immediate successors cautiously built their positions of power by concentrating, as Henry had done in Saxony, on their own areas.

During the first generations of the Capetian kings, the counts and dukes, unhindered, continued their dominance of the political system from their many separate domains. Fragmented geographically, they were united politically in their opposition to central authority in the hands of a king. This was a major characteristic of the 1209

The Medieval Manor

The medieval manor was actually a large self-supporting farming community. The lord who owned all the land subdivided it, retaining one section for himself and distributing the rest among the peasants who lived in the nearby village. In exchange for the right to cultivate their own sections, the peasants had to work the lord's land one or more days a week. They were often forced to pay him a fixed share in kind, as well, usually in grain, poultry, or eggs.

Most soils were quickly exhausted when used for the uninterrupted cultivation of grain. Arable land was generally revitalized by leaving it fallow (unplanted) for some time and then grazing cattle on it. Cultivation and fallowing were often alternated annually in a system of two-course rotation. Sometimes the soil quality was improved by covering the land with peat, cut in the nearby bogs. Both procedures were eventually succeeded by three-course rotation. Summer and winter crops of grain were planted and harvested in succession, followed by a fallow period, after which the cycle was repeated.

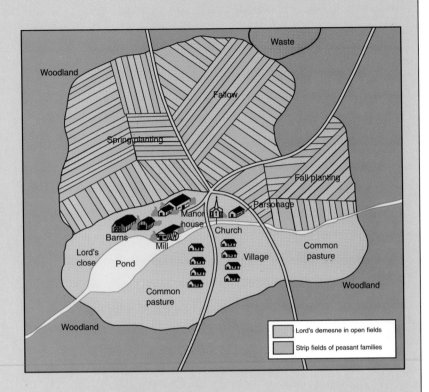

A schematic representation of the layout of a medieval estate

---

feudal system. In the East Frankish Empire, the kings counteracted it, taking advantage of the support offered them by the church to reassert their control.

In the west, Hugh Capet's descendants would rebuild their power on the basis of the principles of heredity, primogeniture, and indivisibility of crown lands. All of these were rooted in the fact that the Capetian kings gained land by marriage. They wanted a way to hold on to it. If landholdings were to remain intact, guaranteed to be passed down undivided through the family, the right to inheritance, first of all, had to be honored. Then, in order not to divide that land, both primogeniture (inheritance by the first son rather than by all) and the indivisibility of land had to be recognized. The first of these concepts, heredity, was used by the Capetians to justify retention of both the crown and their land. It had been invoked by the vassals since the late ninth century in their efforts to retain familial control of the lands they held in fief. The other two ideas were breaches in the all-encompassing system of feudalism, characterized by a mosaic of vying fiefdoms, a powerful nobility, and a weak royalty. The Capetians would undermine that system and rise to dominance by acquiring most of France through the assimilation of additional fiefs into their own lands and then applying these principles.

The Church
In the year 1000, it did not appear to many that the missionaries who had brought Christianity to Europe in prior centuries had established any tradition of deep faith and religious discipline. They had replaced the magical rites of the Germanic tribes with the mysterious liturgy of the church, its Latin prayers, its choral singing, and its holy sacraments. The goal seemed to be to appease a god not all that different from the banished Wodan and his consorts. Only within the walls of some of the monasteries was any notion of the search for a personal god or any tradition of Christian

asceticism and repentance to be found. Even in many monasteries, much of what was done seemed only for the sake of form. Each monastery was autonomous, dependent on the most powerful laymen in the area. The lives of the monks were far from the original ideal. Abuse of privilege was almost routine, many of the prelates anything but fine examples to their parishioners. The papacy was frequently the plaything of various Roman families and, in the Vatican, popes replaced each other with alarming speed. On occasion, civil wars broke out, with two or more popes capturing each others' buildings. If religious offices could not be usurped, they were often sold to the highest bidder, a practice known as *simony,* after Simon Magus (the Magician) who tried to peddle the "magic power" of the apostles for money. One of the few exceptions was Nicholas I, pope from 858 to 867, who proclaimed that Photius, the patriarch of Constantinople, was uncanonically elected. The action set the stage for a schism between the Roman and Byzantine churches.

Over the course of the ninth and tenth centuries, monarchs and noblemen ruled over abbeys and bishoprics, often granting unworthy men the highest spiritual offices. The effect was demoralizing. Reformation was badly needed.

Cluny

Christian laymen and priests did exist who were genuinely concerned about the state of the church. One of these was the West Frankish count William of Aquitaine; another was Berno, a clergyman who was a fierce opponent of the prevailing corruption. In 910, the count bestowed upon Berno the land to found a monastery. From the very beginning, the objective was to create a model community in Burgundy (in east central France) not subject to outside control or the negative influences that were rife in other monasteries. To keep the neighboring bishops and secular lords at bay, William placed Abbot Berno directly under the Holy See, giving up his own control of the monastery to provide total independence in the realization of their shared ideal. They named the monastery Cluny. A major supporter of the concept was Berno's assistant and friend Odo, whom he named as his successor. Abbot Berno died seventeen years after the founding of Cluny. He had created an island of true faith in the midst of a sea of corruption and had established a tradition of independence that would endure for centuries. Odo took

the concept further, founding monasteries throughout Europe on the Cluny model and with its help. They were granted the same status as the parent monastery, except that their abbots were directly accountable to Odo and his successors.

Odo

Odo set forth his theological beliefs in a number of writings, some of which have been preserved. One of these is the epic poem *Occupatio (Occupation)*, a reference to the work of the spirit. In 5,580 hexameter verses (six metric beats per line), the poem details the entire history of Christianity, with explanations and inter-

pretations provided by the author. In Odo's view, the wars, the marauding robbers, the civilian discord, and the hypocrisy within the church all justified his conviction that his own time was the period of the Antichrist. The ideas of eschatology (the branch of theology dealing with last things, death, judgment, and resurrection) made sense to him. He believed that Judgment

Henry II and his wife Kunigunde, shown on a portal of the Bamberg Cathedral in Germany

Day was at hand, the end of the world very near. He wrote that he expected Jesus to return very soon on the clouds. A true faith, he claimed, was therefore essential, so that when the time of final judgment came, one would be saved. Mankind, he insisted, must try to draw closer to its savior, specifically through the practice of the Christian rite of communion, part of every mass (worship service). In this ceremony, worshipers consume a morsel of bread and a sip of wine in remembrance of the last supper Jesus had with his disciples. For

Lance and shield

Helmet

Leg guards

Sword and sheath

Mail shirt

Horse

The cost of a mounted warrior's armor in the ninth century, represented in cows

Odo and Christian believers, this was no symbolic act. The consecrated bread and wine became the body and blood of Christ. This was the essential act to make one closer to Christ, to Odo's way of thinking, but he did not consider communion sufficient on its own. He required a specific attitude toward life, which he called *munditia* (purity), referring to the perfect order of the universe and meaning a kind of purity in body and soul. Believers were to free themselves from attachment to all worldly things and to concentrate on spiritual matters. The concept was not new: The monk Benedict of Nursia had preached it centuries earlier.

Saint Benedict of Nursia (c. 480-547)
Benedict, the son of a noted Italian family, rejected the evils of urban life he saw in Rome and retreated to a cave (later called the Holy Grotto) near Subiaco. He lived there for three years, gaining a reputation as a holy man. He was then asked to head a group of monks in northern Italy, but the monks disliked his stringent policies so much they tried to poison him. He left to found his own monastery at Monte Cassino where he set a standard of monastic life

eventually adopted by most western monasteries.

It was this standard to which Odo returned, insisting on strict asceticism and communal living in his monasteries. Monks were not allowed to own property and were required to avoid unnecessary conversation. Odo thought any speaking in the monastery disturbed the monks' spiritual contemplation. Although he placed great value on silent personal prayer, he did encourage the reciting of prayers. The solemn chants of his monks could be heard day and night from the arched windows of the chapel.

Odo translated his demands of monastic purity into political terms. He contended that the church must be independent of any secular ruler, even the king. No political authority, in his view, should be allowed to interfere in the affairs of the church. Religious authority, on the other hand, should insure that those in positions of secular power conduct themselves according to God's order. The state should be subservient to the church, secular law made according to the papal definition of God's law.

The papal claim to ultimate authority over the empire, based on the Donation of Constantine (as yet unrecognized as a forgery), fit perfectly into this new doctrine. Support for the reform movement and the power of the church increased rapidly. Under Odo's successors, more than two thousand new centers of worship were founded all over Europe. Although Cluny remained paramount, discipline in the outlying monasteries eventually grew less rigorous. Odo came to be regarded as something of a fanatic, but two hundred years later, his thinking would still inform the wisdom of Cluny's most famous abbot, Peter the Venerable.

Early Medieval Politics

Secular Rulers and Papal Power

Otto II (955-983)

Otto II, named king of Germany in 961, ruled as Holy Roman emperor jointly with his father from 967 to 973 and for another ten years on his own. Over that decade, he had to suppress a rebellion initiated by his cousin Henry II, duke of Bavaria, and defend Lorraine against invasion by Lothar, king of France. He staged an unsuccessful seige of Paris as part of this effort, but Lothar eventually renounced Lorraine anyway. In 982, Otto failed again, this time invading Italy. He did manage to take Naples, Salerno, and Taranto before being stopped by the Byzantines and Muslims at Cotrone. He died in Rome in 983, leaving a three-year-old son.

Otto III (980-1002)

The boy, Otto III, was made king of Germany, coregent with his Byzantine mother, Theophano, and his grandmother, Adelaide. In 991, regency authority shifted to a council. In 996, Otto III took control. Crowned as king of Lombardy and as Holy Roman emperor, he set his cousin Bruno on the papal throne as Pope Gregory. When Gregory died, Otto established his own former tutor Gerbert as Pope

A bishop, with scepter and miter, offering benediction; eleventh-century sculpture

Sylvester II. The emperor dreamed of a Christendom united to meet both secular and spiritual needs. He wanted to restore some of the customs of ancient Rome and worked to make the city the capital of the Holy Roman Empire.

Otto III stayed in Rome until he died, leaving no direct descendants. The aristocracy was required to make the royal choice for the first time in nearly a century.

Henry the Saint (973-1024)

The nobles granted the crown to Otto's nearest relative, Duke Henry of Bavaria, to their later regret. Henry II, last of the Saxon rulers, was German king from 1002 to 1024. In 1004, he invaded Italy and was also made king of the Lombards. In that year, as well, he began a fourteen-year battle with Boleslav I, king of Poland, regaining the German territory of Bohemia in 1018. He convinced Rudolf III, king of

1213

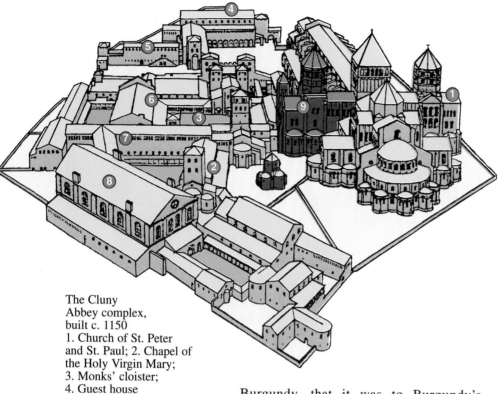

The Cluny Abbey complex, built c. 1150
1. Church of St. Peter and St. Paul; 2. Chapel of the Holy Virgin Mary; 3. Monks' cloister; 4. Guest house; 5. Lay brothers' residence; 6. *Refectorium* (monks' dining hall); 7. *Dormitorium* (monks' dormitory); 8. Hospital; 9. Only remaining section of the medieval abbey church.

Burgundy, that it was to Burgundy's advantage to join Germany when Rudolf died.

In 1014, Henry was crowned emperor by Pope Benedict VIII. Four years later, at the request of that pope, Henry mounted a third expedition to southern Italy, acquiring Capua and Salerno. Throughout his empire, he was making nobles unhappy. They were used to Otto's style of rule, from a distance in Italy.

Above all else, the nobles objected to Henry for his piety. A church reformer, he drove the nobility from the bishoprics and established a number of church-run monasteries and schools. He would be canonized (declared a saint) in 1146. When he died in 1024, a sworn enemy of the church renewal movement was chosen to replace him: Duke Conrad of Franconia, a descendant of Otto the Great.

Conrad II (990?-1039)

Founder of the Franconian, or Salian, dynasty, Conrad was king of Germany from 1024 to his death in 1039. Crowned king of the Lombards in 1026, he spent a year quashing rebellion in northern Italy before he was crowned Holy Roman emperor by the pope.

He inherited the kingdom of Burgundy from Rudolf III. An important link between the German and Italian parts of the empire, this significantly enlarged his holdings and his prestige. No less imperious than his predecessor, the new emperor also had to contend with uprisings among the nobility. He adopted an unusual means to deal with them: he supported the lower nobles, the vassals, against the tribal dukes. With their help, he was able to secure direct rule over most of the duchies. Only Saxony and the chaotic Lorraine were able to stay free. Conrad's position now became so strong that he was able to secure his son's succession without the necessity of an election. The pattern of a hereditary crown in the house of Conrad would continue for a century.

Henry III the Black (1017-1056)

This political continuity, made possible by the support of the church, was initiated by Conrad's son Henry, moving away from the paternal antipope policies. Henry's reformation efforts, particularly his donation of large areas of land to monasteries and individual prelates, got him named German king in 1028 and Holy Roman emperor in 1039. Busy defending his Polish vassals against invading Bohemians and then restoring the deposed Hungarian king to power, Henry did not go to Rome until 1046. He then undertook to put an

Section of the cloister of the present-day monastery at Cluny, with the octagonal tower of the twelfth-century abbey church in the background

end to the conflict caused by three rival contenders for the papacy.

The debauched and brutal pope Benedict IX had abdicated and given his office to a wealthy supporter of the renewal movement for an unknown sum. This pope, named Gregory VI, began to use his fortune to rid the church of decay, adopting simony (the sale of church office) to ban-

ish corruption, even though simony was a form of corruption. Benedict, now regretting his move, attempted to rule from the Lateran palace, while Gregory barricaded himself into Santa Maria Maggiore. In the meantime, a third pretender had returned to Rome: Sylvester III, pawn of a Roman family, took over St. Peter's.

Henry III possessed not only the will but the power to act. He deposed all three rivals and appointed the German bishop of Bamberg the next pope. Now called Clement II, the new pope promptly crowned Henry Holy Roman emperor. Over the rest of his reign, Henry would appoint three succeeding popes, all Germans. The papacy was once more in the hands of the emperor.

Henry's version of reformation met with much resistance. The supporters of Gregory VI still dreamed of a free church without lay custodians, however reform-

minded they might be. One of the most influential of these was Gregory's chaplain, Hildebrand. In 1059, they drew up a scheme for electing the pope by a college of Roman clergymen (later cardinals), subject to approval by the people of Rome. This was clearly an attempt to escape the influence of the emperor and the nobility.

The Investiture Controversy: Emperor Henry IV versus Pope St. Gregory VII

The fiercest spokesman for an independent church continued to be the Tuscan monk Hildebrand (circa 1020-1085). In 1073, while the college of cardinals was preparing to elect a new pope, the people put him on the papal throne by acclamation. He took the name Gregory VII to honor his illustrious namesake. His efforts both before and after this election comprise what is called the Gregorian Reform. He asserted the primacy of the church over

The imperial crown of the Holy Roman Empire, made up of a cross, a diadem, and eight connected plates, all set with jewels

1215

Otto III (980-1002)

Detail of a column in the Church of St. Bartholomew in Rome depicting Emperor Otto III

Born in Kessel, Germany, Otto III was the son of Otto II, who died when Otto III was three years old. The toddler was made king of Germany in 983. His mother, Theophano, and his grandmother, Adelaide, served as his coregents until 994. Theophano, a Greek, taught him to read and write and instilled in him an interest in culture. The boy's aunt, Mathilde, the abbess of a German convent, also played a large role in his upbringing. Otto III ruled under the regency of a council from 991 to 996, when he was crowned king of the Lombards and took power on his own. He went to Rome where he remained until his death, a fact indicative of his policy to make the city the capital of the Holy Roman Empire and to restore many of the customs of the ancient Roman Empire. He installed his cousin Bruno as Pope Gregory VI.

Otto III was crowned emperor in Rome in 998 at the age of nineteen. Following Pope Gregory's death in 999, he had his own former tutor, Gerbert, elected pope as Sylvester II. He dreamed of ruling over all Christendom with the new pope and fantasized about *a renovatio imperii,* a revitalization of the empire. Like his mother, he attempted to establish a Byzantine-style court, which was resented in Rome. His goal was to bring about a reconciliation between the Latin and the Byzantine Christians, to form an empire headed by himself and his Byzantine counterpart as coemperors.

Constantinople refused to cooperate, however. From his coronation onward, Otto was thwarted continuously by the Byzantines and increasingly unpopular even with his own subjects. His historical significance lies not in his inconclusive wars with the Slavs and the Italians, but in his dreams of a renewed Christian empire, the imperial ideal of medieval feudal society.

secular authority, leading the church against the might of the Holy Roman Empire.

Henry IV (1050-1106) had succeeded his father three years prior to this, at the age of six. His mother acted as regent until he came of age in 1065. Almost at once he had to quell a rebellion in Saxony. He could not afford to antagonize the pope as well.

Gregory made good use of Henry's weakness, putting through strong reforms in the Roman Synod of 1075 to eliminate simony, to promote clerical celibacy, and to forbid both the appointment of church officials and lay investiture by secular rulers. He regarded investiture (the conferring upon prelates of the symbols of their

Miniature from Trier (Germany) depicting Emperor Otto II receiving tribute from the four provinces of his empire

After the fall of the Roman Empire, Western Christianity survived only in Ireland and Italy. The Chalice of Ardagh (Ireland) from the eighth or ninth century, made of bronze and gold, is shown here.

religious authority) as an exclusive church right. The synod formalized the outbreak of the investiture controversy, the papal-imperial struggle for authority over the church. The controversy itself was not new. Secular nobility had virtually taken over the appointment of the clergy at every level. Large landowners who had founded an abbey on their land or who had built a church for one of their villages saw it as only fair that they should appoint the people to run it. Kings used the same logic. They had to protect the religious institutions within the kingdom and, in the middle ages, the protector was the patron. The rite of investiture was the most visible symbol of authority and thus the first regulation that Gregory targeted for attack. He demanded the abolition of lay investiture and the reintroduction of traditional election to church positions by the clergy and laypeople in the bishoprics. The pope further reprimanded Henry for appointing prelates in Italy.

Henry IV convened a German council at Worms to depose the pope in 1076, sending him a letter addressed to "the false monk Hildebrand." The pope responded by excommunicating the emperor and declaring him anathema. This meant that the emperor was totally excluded from the community of believers and that no one was obliged to keep any oaths made to Henry. The act released his subjects from any allegiance to him, seriously undermining his authority. The only way back was through papal forgiveness.

The nobles formed a coalition, threatening not to recognize Henry unless he secured absolution by February 1077. There were even plans for a diet, which would be chaired by Gregory. If Henry did not receive forgiveness by the time it met, he would be deposed. Only reconciliation with the pope could save him.

Canossa

Henry left for Italy in the middle of

autumn. In January, he arrived at the castle of Canossa, where the pope had taken up residence. Clad in a rough hair shirt and standing barefoot in the snow, he prayed and fasted in front of the gates for three days in the cold. Only then did Gregory let him in, probably reluctantly. By his own theological convictions, he could do nothing but forgive the repentant sinner, but this was what saved Henry's throne.

"We are not going to go to Canossa," the German chancellor Bismarck is quoted as saying eight hundred years later, meaning that he would not yield to his Catholic opponents, acknowledging defeat. The adage, however, is open to interpretation. Henry's journey, appeared to be a tremendous defeat, the lowest point in the history of his house. Had he, in fact, cleverly put Gregory in political checkmate? The pope could never refuse absolution to a repentant sinner. Henry only had to show contrition, nothing else, not even goodwill.

The conflict was not yet over. The German nobles did meet. They elected Rudolf, duke of Swabia, to replace Henry IV, which caused a civil war. In 1080, the pope recognized the kingship of Rudolf, again excommunicating Henry. There was no second Canossa. Henry won the civil war, which gave him the opportunity to settle his score with Gregory. He declared Pope Gregory deposed and had the Italian archbishop Guibert of Ravenna elected as Pope Clement III. Rudolf was killed in 1080, which allowed Henry to reestablish control in Germany.

In 1084, Henry IV captured Rome and was crowned emperor by Clement III. His army drove Gregory and his followers to Salerno, where the Normans held sway. A Norman army came to the aid of Pope Gregory and, in turn, drove Henry from Rome. Back in Germany, Henry became embroiled in civil war, with even his sons against him. Taken prisoner by his son Henry in 1105, he was forced to abdicate. He escaped the next year, only to die trying to form yet another army.

The pontificate (or papal reign) of the man who was the political arch rival of Henry IV, Pope Gregory VII, was perhaps the most controversial in history. He reinforced the principles of Christianity, establishing the foundation on which to base a reinvigorated church. He insisted on ecclesiastical rather than imperial dominance of church institutions. He was canonized in 1606 as Saint Gregory VII.

Henry V (1086-1125)

Henry V had been German king since 1098,

when he imprisoned his father out of fear that he might never be made Holy Roman emperor. In 1106, when Henry IV died, his son received the crown he so coveted undisputed, if only for a time.

In 1110, the issue of lay investiture sur-

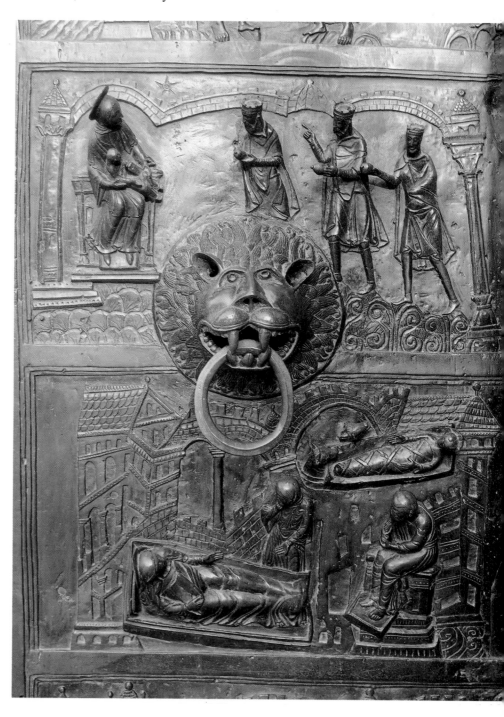

faced again. Henry V offered to honor the decree of Pope Paschal II against the practice if the pope would crown him and turn over its secular holdings to him. This bargain, only made known on the coronation day, was completely rejected by the clergy. The pope abruptly refused to crown Henry, who, in turn, took the pope prisoner. Paschal then changed his mind, not only crowning Henry but granting him the

Section of a bronze door in the cathedral at Hildesheim (built 1010-1015). The adoration of the kings is depicted at the top.

Emperor Henry III
and his wife,
Agnes of Poitiers, honor
the Virgin Mary.
Miniature from the *Codex
Aureus (Golden Code
or Gospels)* of the
eleventh century

power of investiture. Two years later, the pope retracted everything.

Over the next several years, most of the German princes revolted against Henry V. He invaded Rome anyway, drove out Pope Paschal, and had himself recrowned in 1117 by Maurice Bourdin, the archbishop of Braga. Paschal died in 1118; Henry V then declared the archbishop as the antipope Gregory VIII. This led to Henry's

excommunication by Paschal's legitimate successor, Pope Gelasius II.

At the Diet of Würzburg in 1121, Henry V made peace with the princes, finally ending the German civil wars. A year later, he did the same with the papacy.

Concordat of Worms (1122)

Henry V and the incumbent Pope Calixtus II signed a treaty (or concordat) in Worms in 1122 that set out precise rules for investiture. In Italy and Burgundy, the bishops and abbots were to receive their spiritual regalia from a superior of the church. Only after that would they receive their secular regalia from a representative of the emperor. Elsewhere, the exact opposite was to take place. Abbots and bishops were to receive the secular regalia first, followed by the ecclesiastical symbols. Abandoning the antipope Gregory VIII, Henry was reinstated in the church. No longer allowed to impose his appointments, he still retained the right to the deciding vote in the "chapters," ecclesiastical colleges established to elect new bishops. The chapters increasingly filled with the sons of regional noble houses, who used them to increase their own power. In practice, the emperor could still exert considerable influence.

During his last year as emperor, in alliance with his father-in-law, Henry I of England, Henry V would lead an unsuccessful expedition against Louis VI of France. Henry V died in Utrecht in 1125, the last of the Salian emperors.

Theocracy

The compromise reached in the Concordat of Worms was highly controversial, giving rise to a flood of publications on the subject. There were fundamental differences in the theological views and political theories of the era.

An important part of the conflict had to do with worldview, literally how one pictured the universe. Looked at diagrammatically, it was the pyramid versus the pair of circles: the concept of the emperor at the top of the pyramid, God's deputy on earth to rule over all things spiritual and secular alike, versus the concept of two separate powers (depicted as circles) in the universe, the spiritual and the secular, or the sacred and the profane. The clergy was responsible for the spiritual world and the emperor for the secular. In this view, they were expected to work together for the common good of mankind.

Early in the investiture debate (investiture symbolizing the authority to choose who ran the church), a different notion was advanced by the papacy. In effect, it was the pyramid view with the pope at the top, not the emperor. The theory suggested that the pope was given both religious and secular power by God, that he was responsible for both, and that he should, therefore, delegate secular power to a worthy ruler. This was theocracy, rule by those presuming to have divine authority. Pope Gregory VII

was a particular advocate of this view, in both its political and its theological aspects.

To the imperial bloc, this meant that the pope was claiming the power to appoint the emperor, something that only God was deemed to possess.

To the ecclesiastical bloc, the new theory raised yet another question. Its proponents replaced the term *clergy* with *pope*.

The implication was that it was the pope himself, not the clergy acting as a body, who held highest authority. The position of the pope within the church itself, the power of the papacy, became a second important aspect of the conflict. The controversy was no longer just about the issue of church and state. It had moved to a question of church and church, the authority of the pope in Rome against that of the patri-

Emperor Henry IV talking to Countess Mathilde and Abbot Hugh of Cluny, whom he asked to mediate for him with Pope Gregory VII

Interior text labels on woodcut (Latin inscriptions):

papa PRSOKE MABEBTE · De vovet expvlsvs clerv
heinricvs iii Gvz —bertvs Gregori vii
Eu Fides Scissor · evm Rege Forete +
hic crviceoz paret ovrabizss evz.
Gregorivs vii Gregorivs vii moritvr.

The upper section of this twelfth-century woodcut shows Pope Gregory VII being deposed by Emperor Henry IV and the antipope, Clement III. The lower left section shows Gregory being liberated by the Normans; the lower right, his death in 1085.

Interior of the Abbey Church at Reichenau, Germany, built in the ninth and tenth centuries. Many of the tenth- and eleventh-century murals have survived.

archate in Constantinople. Pope Gregory demanded greater centralization of authority in the papacy.

The Great Schism (1054)

There was nothing new about tension between Constantinople and Rome. It had existed at least since the fall of Rome in AD 476 when the pope (the bishop of Rome, by his Byzantine title) was left the protector of western Christianity. Rome was the burial place of the apostle Peter, according to the Bible *(Matthew 16:18),* the "rock" on which the church was to be built. Roman popes claimed direct succession to Peter and therefore "apostolic" primacy, authority above any ecumenical council.

The patriarchate of Constantinople respected that tradition, permitting the Roman bishop some authority because they contended that the rights of any church were determined by historical factors. They held that their own position gave them top rank because Constantinople was the seat of the Byzantine emperor and the church senate,

Lavishly decorated manuscript from c. 1050. The gospel text is written in gold, rather than ink. The miniature depicts the Last Supper.

actual or "pragmatic" historical factors. These two centuries-old views of primacy, apostolic versus pragmatic, were debated again in the eleventh century.

There were other long-standing issues, as well. In the seventh century in Spain, the Latin word *filioque,* meaning "and from the Son," was used to interpolate (expand, alter, or corrupt, depending on one's viewpoint here) the accepted creed (or statement of religious belief). It now read: "I believe 'in the Holy Spirit' who proceeds from the Father and from the Son." This interpolation or alteration of the words was opposed by Rome until about 1014, despite the fact that the Emperor

Charlemagne accepted and promoted it as early as 800. In Byzantium (or Constantinople), it was considered heretical. Other concerns were the fact that, only in the East, married men could be ordained as priests and unleavened bread could be used in the rite of Holy Communion.

Page from the *Codex Aureus (Golden Code* or *Gospels)*. Emperor Conrad II and his wife are shown kneeling before Christ.

These theological issues could not be settled because of the one that dominated them all: the ultimate source of judgment. The papacy claimed itself infallible, the final authority, while the East invoked a conciliar principle, the authority of councils in which even local churches had equal voice.

All the centuries of disagreements led to an exchange of anathemas between the patriarch Michael Cerularius I and papal legates in Constantinople in 1054 called the Great Schism.

The Role of the Reform Movement

The split has been frequently attributed to the influence of the reform-minded popes who insisted that the Byzantine church accept the apostolic primacy and the doctrine of the papacy. There was important political reason for it, as well, evident in the apparent paradox of the investiture controversy in Germany: a considerable number of bishops supported the emperor, while many noblemen supported the pope. If the emperor had the right to clerical appointments, it behooved the clergy to support him. If the pope had that right, it undermined imperial power and strengthened that of the nobles. The pope's insistence on the end of lay investiture struck at the local foundations of the emperor's power even as his demand for the authority of imperial appointment threatened on high.

The reform movement was a catalyst in the social change of an era. The church had previously placed great emphasis on stability, regarding it as of inherent value whether in matters of social structure, its own organization, or religious values. The reform popes transformed that attitude, recognizing the necessity of change and creating a demand for it. Clergymen who had been granted their positions by secular authorities were now subject to criticism. Support was even given to civil uprisings against bishops of the old order. There was genuine effort made in the monasteries to encourage piety on the Clunaic model.

Developments of this nature encouraged the ordinary layman to start speaking up. It would not be long before critical ideas on the clergy would start developing among the laity that went a lot further than the reformers of the Roman church wanted. New ideas would arise not focused on the political and institutional problems of the church but on the biblical description of the *vita apostolica* (apostolic life), living as the apostles did.

The model church, the ideal of Odo and Hildebrand, had not been achieved, but a number of important steps had been taken in that direction. The Roman church had gained a significant amount of freedom, with the pope as its powerful spokesman. He would continue to try to establish himself as the head of the church. It would soon become apparent that he required the support of the secular nobility.

The interior of the mosque at Córdoba, famous for its colorful arches

The Muslims

Rule in Spain

Islamic presence on the Iberian Peninsula began with the 711 invasion by Tariq ibn-Ziyad and his Berber Muslim army. Crossing the Strait of Gibraltar from North Africa, they conquered the Visigoth kingdom and ran north to the Pyrenees Mountains. They established a dependency of the province of North Africa, itself part of the caliphate of Damascus. By 717, the Moors, as the conquerors were pejoratively called, yielded direct rule (or misrule) to officials called emirs, appointed by the caliphs. (Twenty emirs would have to be appointed over the next forty years, they were so inept.) The Muslims held the entire peninsula except for Asturias and the Basque country. Their advance was only stopped in France in 732 by the Frankish king Charles Martel.

A conflict for control of the empire in Spain and North Africa arose between the Umayyad and Abbasid dynasties. Claiming descent from Abbas, the uncle of Muhammad, the Abbasids began ruling Baghdad in 750. (They would continue to do so until 1258.) The last of their Spanish emirs, Yusuf, favored the Abbasids, but powerful local officials supported the Umayyads. The Umayyad faction invited one of their own, 'Abd ar-Raḥmōn I (731-788), to become the independent ruler of Spain. In 756, he overrode the feud, captured Córdoba, and founded an independent hereditary emirate.

Viewed from the glory of Baghdad in 912, this emirate was unimportant. There, although the muezzin (crier) called faithful Muslims to prayer from the minarets (tow-

Section of a rug made by eleventh-century Muslim artists in Seville.
It was presented as a gift to Christians.

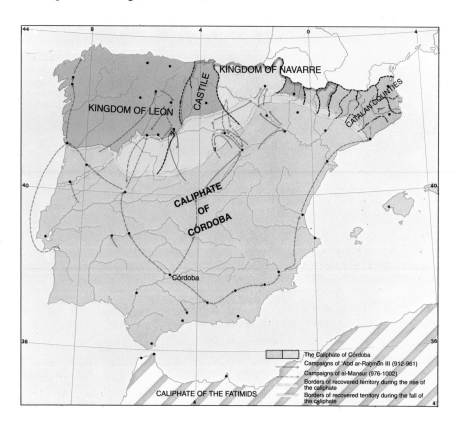

Map shows
the developments
within the caliphate of
Córdoba between
929 and 1031.

emir himself wanted to be independent from the Abbasid domination in Damascus.

'Abd ar-Raḥmōn III asserted Umayyad control throughout the peninsula and beyond. Creating a naval fleet unequaled anywhere, he had it sail to Morocco to seize land from the Fatimids. In 929, he confidently proclaimed himself caliph, leader of all believers. From then on, he took the name al-Nasir li-din Allah, victorious warrior for the faith of Allah: He developed his small emirate on the edge of the Arabian Empire into one of the largest centers of Islamic civilization.

In the northern part of the Iberian Peninsula, the Christian Visigoths still held their own against him. Invited in to aid the Romans against invaders in AD 412, the Visigoths had been there ever since. The Visigothic kingdom of Toulouse, nominally under Rome, had dispersed Roman culture and Christianity for three centuries. Roderick, last of the Toulouse kings, was defeated by the Berbers at the Battle of Río Barbate in 711. The small Christian kingdom of Asturias, founded on the northern peninsula about 718 by Pelayo, a Visigothic chieftain, replaced Toulouse in importance. Pelayo's son-in-law took over virtually all of Galicia and León and was crowned Alfonso I, king of León and Asturias. Alfonso III greatly expanded the kingdom in the early tenth century, about

ers) and the pious bowed five times a day toward Mecca (the holy city of Islam), the Umayyad ruler had no real influence. Eighth and last Umayyad emir in succession, 'Abd ar-Raḥmōn III (889-961) inherited an emirate fragmented by provincial governors each insisting on autonomy. The

the time Navarre became an independent Christian kingdom under Sancho I. The León kings continued east to Burgos, building castles to guard their frontiers: the region came to be called Castilla, or Castile. In 932, Count Fernán González declared it independent of León and himself its first king. 'Abd ar-Raḥmōn III halted the expansion of each of these Christian kingdoms. Tenant farmers and lords alike dreamed of a *reconquista*, a reconquering of their lands from the conquerors of a different faith. However, Spanish civilization under the Muslims was far more advanced than that in the rest of Europe.

Muslim Civilization

The Prophet Muhammad, founder of Islam, was originally a merchant in Mecca; hence, the importance of that city to Islam. His revelations are compiled in the Koran, central to Islamic culture. Its importance and the particular beauty of written Arabic led to the use of Koranic inscriptions in mosques and the development of calligraphic ornament in Islamic art.

Iberian Muslims were highly educated, building great universities and free schools for the poor. They studied mathematics, astronomy, and medicine as well as the liberal arts. The Greek philosophers were familar to them before they were even known in Christian Europe. Literature, art, and architecture flourished.

They developed agriculture, constructing systems of irrigation in the south. Integrated into the Arabian economy of dirhams and dinars, they opened the Mediterranean to trade with the Orient. Spanish products, fine cloth, or magnificent swords from Toledo were very popular there. Politically, they were tolerant of dissenters. As long as the Christians did not build churches that were too imposing, they could go their own way undisturbed. Córdoba even had its own bishop.

The Capital

'Abd ar-Raḥmōn III made Córdoba the capital of his caliphate, transforming it into a splendid cultural center that would rival Baghdad and Constantinople for the next two hundred years. Including its neighboring communities, the city had half a million inhabitants in the tenth century. Its *souks* (markets) bustled with Arabs, Berbers, Visigoths, Africans, Franks, Jews, and Muslims from all over the world.

The commercial district stretched out around the enormous mosque built in the eighth century. Storekeepers displayed their wares in the narrow streets, those in the same trade grouped together, tanners in one street, bakers in another, and booksellers in another. The better shops had their own courtyards so that distinguished clients could get away from the bustle of the street. These shops often had hotels on the second floor, where buyers from out of

Front and back of a dinar coined during the reign of caliph Hisham II

Ruins of al-Zahra, the city built near Córdoba by 'Abd ar-Raḥmōn III, after he had himself proclaimed caliph. Al-Zahra became the residence of the court and seat of government.

1227

One of the entrance doors to the throne room of the Aljafaria (palace) in Zaragoza

when a night watchman was put on every street, complete with dog and lamp, the city remained dangerous.

The mosque *La Mezquita,* with its great dome high above the roofs of the surrounding sea of houses, was viewed as the center of the realm. Every Friday, the caliph preached a sermon here. The state treasury was kept here. Estimated at twenty million dinar in the tenth century, it later turned out to be double that amount.

Taxes

The money was raised by taxes. The palace mathematicians had developed a well-oiled tax system, based on the policies of the first caliphs. All subjects paid tithes and land tax. Non-Muslims had to pay a poll tax in addition to this. Duty on imports and exports and certain market license fees brought in huge sums, as did the tribute the caliph demanded from all states under his influence. There was also a profitable inheritance law: the property of anyone dying without heirs went to the state. Various state monopolies provided further income to the treasury. All finances were managed by the caliph but he maintained a strict division between his private income and that of the state. His private income was quite impressive. Caliph al-Hakam received so much from his personal holdings that he was able to distribute a quarter of his annual profits to Córdoba's poor. The treasury had offices throughout the realm. In each provincial capital, a *kadi* would determine how to allocate the money he had been provided for welfare and public buildings. Impressive architecture gracing many Spanish cities gives an indication of the huge scale and the bold approach that characterized Muslim architecture.

Administration

Through the centuries, the Umayyads perfected palace administration. A balanced hierarchy existed. When 'Abd ar-Raḥmōn III died, 3,750 people were employed in the palace, each with a precise job description. All were under the authority of the fatas, or head slaves. No fewer than 6,500 people lived in the harem, primarily the women and the eunuchs who were their guards and servants. The highest officials were given the honorary title of *vizier.* Their power was limited to specific functions. In contrast to Baghdad where the grand vizier held a key position, his Spanish counterparts were sometimes given sinecures with no real content.

The most important government official under the caliph was called the *hagib.* He

town could spend the night. The most powerful person in the commercial district was the *mustasib,* a government official who made sure the traders complied with the law. He was supposed to prevent fraud and to monitor the quality of merchandise.

The reports written by the mustasibs offer a fascinating glimpse into nightlife in Córdoba. Despite a large civil guard, robbery and murder were common. Even

had constant access to the sovereign. He supervised both the army and civil government, which made him extraordinarily powerful—so powerful that the many lesser rulers who later divided the state of Córdoba would call themselves hagib.

The caliph lived in stately seclusion with his officials, generally only appearing on Fridays to preach his weekly sermon in the mosque. Occasionally, he attended special ceremonies with his *hassa*, or retinue.

Because the caliph's power rested on the oath of allegiance, the most important ceremony to a new ruler was the one where he received it. That ceremony took place very soon after the death of a caliph. Just one day after 'Abd ar-Raḥmōn III died, his son sent emissaries to invite everyone to the ceremony. He personally received the oath from his two highest-ranking officials immediately. They were then able to hear the oaths of subordinates in his name while

View of the decoration above the entrance to the prayer chapel of the Aljafaria, built in the eleventh century

A decorated ivory box used to store valuables and perfume. Many boxes like this were stolen from mosques and presented to churches during the *Reconquista*.

A wooden box with gold and silver fittings. Because Islam forbid the portrayal of people on religious objects, Muslim artists frequently used symmetrical abstract patterns instead.

he received court dignitaries. After they swore allegiance, his eight brothers had their turn, followed by the viziers. Then all took their places around the throne to let the people take the oath. Only after the ceremony was over could 'Abd ar-Raḥmōn III be buried.

Decline

Within a century of his proclamation, 'Abd ar-Raḥmōn III's caliphate lay in ruins. A civil uprising in Córdoba drove the last

Back and front of a dirham coined during the time of the Almoravids (1086-1146)

Umayyad, the drunkard Hisham III, into exile. His hagibs, the most prominent members of staff and the ministers of government, as was customary, had been taken from families with literally a century of experience. With his death in 1036, they now divided the caliphate into a number of independent and harshly competitive kingdoms: Córdoba, Granada, Lisbon, Zaragoza, Seville, Murcia, Valencia, and Toledo.

The Almoravids

The breakup permitted a resurgence of Christian influence in northern Spain, as the waiting Christian kings went into action. This led to the formation of strange coalitions that crossed religious lines. There were Christian noblemen who fought for Muslims and Christian rulers who rescued hagibs. Alfonso I of Castile led an army south and conquered Toledo in 1086. This threatened Seville where the Muslim Abbadids had returned to power in 1023. Abbad al-Mutamid, called Abbad III of Seville, turned to a Muslim sect in the Moroccan Atlas mountains of North Africa, the Almoravids, for assistance. They entered Spain and defeated Alfonso on Abbad's behalf in 1086. The Almoravids saw themselves as reformers, prepared to spread their Koranic convictions with the argument of the sword. They saw the luxury in the cities, the unveiled women, and the lax enforcement of Muhammad's laws. They turned around and attacked the Seville Muslims. By 1091, they had taken over Seville and had established their righteous kingdom. By the turn of the century, they ruled all Muslim Spain.

In worldly Córdoba, however, it turned out to be impossible to sustain their ideology. In the magnificent palace of the Umayyads, the Almoravid caliphs fell into the pleasures of wine drinking and other Islamic sins. Less than a century later, a second reform movement tried to restore Allah's religion to its original form.

The Almohads

A second African sect, the Almohads, invaded Spain in 1145 to wage *jihad* (holy war) against the degenerate Almoravids. Under their *mahdi* (or redeemer), they had already spread throughout northern Africa. They did so now in Spain, gaining control of all Muslim areas within five years and establishing an aggressive caliphate. The Christian kings of the northern territories, meanwhile, backed by their long-repressed people, had joined forces and kept on their southbound conquests. At once political and religious opponents, the Christian and Muslim armies met in a final battle in July 1212, on the plains of Toledo. The united Christians won, driving the Almohads out of Spain altogether soon after. The Muslims had been defeated, their influence restricted to the harbor region around Cádiz and the small mountain kingdom of Granada. This lasted until 1492, one of the most magnificent places in the Islamic world.

The rest of Spain was divided into two great kingdoms during the thirteenth, fourteenth, and fifteenth centuries: Castile and León (including Asturias, Córdoba, Estremadura, Galicia, Jaén, and Seville) and Aragon (including Barcelona, Valencia, and the Balearic Islands). All had a variety of languages, peoples (Christians, Muslims, and Jews), and political forms.

The Recon- quista

The Recovery of the West

Fresco of Alfonso I, founder of the kingdom of Asturias. Alfonso was responsible for initiating the Reconquista.

As early as the tenth century, there were signs that Latin Christianity would transcend its crises, that it would be able to achieve internal reform and to withstand external attack. The trend would gain momentum in the eleventh century as widespread political anarchy gradually gave way to stability.

At the Battle of Lechfield in the Eastern Frankish Empire in 955, Otto of Germany ended the threat of Magyar invasion to Europe. Seven years later, he was crowned Holy Roman emperor by Pope John XII. Although the two subsequently initiated a conflict between the papacy and the emperorship that would last a century, Otto managed to take control of both Italy and Germany. His dynasty established a relatively stable regime with the help of the state bishops.

In the Western Frankish Empire in the tenth century, royal authority still counted for little, but the incessant rivalry characteristic of the feudal era began to subside as regional leaders increasingly took control of their own territories. Most notable among these were the counts of Anjou and Flanders and the dukes of Normandy and Aquitaine.

As political stability improved with the turn of the century, so did the economic sector. Agriculture, virtually the only economic activity in the early Middle Ages, expanded rapidly. Vacant swampland was drained and dammed for cultivation. Forests were cut down to make fields. A wider application of the three-field system (one field each for early and late harvests; the third lying fallow to regenerate) made much larger harvests possible. The implementation of new agricultural techniques, especially the introduction of the heavy plow, improved crop yield. Fewer people were necessary to farm, yet more food was produced.

An increasing number of people, released from direct agricultural production, began to develop new occupations and industries during the eleventh century. This, coupled with continual population growth, led to the gradual emergence of cities. These had their own economic functions. Here, specialized processing of agri-

Section of an embroidered standard carried by the Almohad armies in the battle at Las Navas de Tolosa (1212). The defeat they suffered there signaled the beginning of the Almohadan decline.

cultural products took place, the most important being textile production. This, in turn, gave fresh impetus to trade, especially north of the Alps, where annual fairs began to play an increasingly important role. Interregional commerce had been almost nonexistent until the tenth century, when ships from the coastal cities of Amalfi, Salerno, and Venice began to ply the trade routes of the Mediterranean.

With the general improvement of society came a noticeable sense of religious optimism among the Christians and a revival of popular faith in the established church. The Christian world blossomed with new churches. Prominent members of society considered themselves God's tools, busily establishing His kingdom on earth. They saw God primarily as the helper of the worthy rather than the punisher of the sinful. Reformation movements like that at Cluny, with their pleas for a religion that meant more than a set of rituals, had begun to set the tone for the church. Since Gregory VII, such ideas had become the aggressive guidelines of papal policy, moving far beyond an appeal for intensified faith within the church to a demand for the cleansing of un-Christian elements from society. Combining new forms of religious and political activity, this church initiative became known as the Peace of God movement.

The Peace of God Movement
The main victims of the anarchy that prevailed under feudalism had always been the noncombatants, serfs and priests alike. The rich monasteries were easy prey. The tangle of conflicts among the feudal lords had precipitated a profusion of raids and arson no longer tolerable to general society in the eleventh century. The meager political establishment was unable to stop the lords from fighting their petty private wars. Other methods had to be found.

The church itself stepped in. It developed a code of honor, called the Peace of God, for Christian warriors. Aimed specifically at the vying feudal nobility, it required the warriors to spare and protect the weaker members of society in general, widows, orphans, and priests in particular. It even mandated the times of battle: no fighting was allowed between Wednesday and Sunday evening. Anyone not adhering to this code of honor was committing a sin. Violations were dealt with in special ecclesiastical courts or synods.

The players on the battlefields varied like pieces in a game of chess. Farmers led by their priests would march on the fortresses of their feudal masters, only to be countered by kings and powerful vassals attempting to improve their own positions. One of the biggest problems of the great landowning magnates was keeping their own pugnacious vassals in control. Because they granted land in fief to those vassals, it was very much in their own financial interest to allow them some freedom to

UBIEXPUGNANSIBESLAD.

Detail from
a tenth-century Spanish
manuscript, depicting
cavalry and infantry of a
Christian army

act. The landlords would be accorded shares of any lands or plunder seized. Yet they also sought to regain full possession of the fiefs they had granted and to limit local vassal autonomy.

Given their shared concern, an informal alliance arose between the church and the most important magnates and princes for the purpose of preserving the Peace of God. They now declared that anyone violating the peace not only committed a sin against his god but reneged on his feudal obligations to his earthly lord, thereby forfeiting his rights as a vassal.

Partly owing to the development of the Peace of God, the church became further involved in issues of war and peace. It developed an ideal for warriors, a code of chivalry based on religious standards and values. It stipulated, for example, that an aspirant to knighthood had to spend the night before he was dubbed in a church in religious meditation. The concept of just warfare was modified to support the notion that war could only be justified if carried out in defense of Christendom. This won popular support very quickly. The concept turned out to be open to interpretation: it could validate wars of conquest outside present borders, whether to recapture lost territory or to attack as the best form of defense.

In the east, Christian German colonists drove back the pagan Slavs, beating a path from the Elbe to the Oder River and beyond. They established new cities and kingdoms on the conquered territory, founding influential bishoprics for the church that capitalized on the *Drang nach Osten* (rush to the east), which had already been underway for a century.

In the Mediterranean area, a formidable offensive developed that would reverberate in all the Latin Christian territories. The pope added his blessing and support to it, encouraging the faithful to support the warriors for the gospel and for the recovery of Christian territory. The fact that greed and faith went hand in hand at the enemy borders only offered extra incentive. Many Christians joined the efforts to expand the dominance of their religion, to great success. For the first time, to their amazement, they put the Muslims in Spain and the south of Italy on the defensive.

Spain

As the eleventh century opened, five small Christian kingdoms existed on the Iberian Peninsula. From east to west, these were León, Castile, Navarre, Catalan Aragon, and Barcelona.

León's history was linked with that of Asturias, which had flourished from the eighth to the tenth centuries in northwest Spain. The Iberian Muslims had occupied León during the eighth century until its reconquest by Alfonso III, king of

Statue
of Ordoño II,
king of Asturias
in the ninth
century

Asturias. In 910, Alfonso III abdicated. Asturias was partitioned among his three sons. León became an independent Christian kingdom.

Sancho III, king of Navarre, seized a large part of Aragon from the Muslims and went on to conquer León and Castile. In 1033 he made his son, Ferdinand I, king of Castile. This temporary unity came to an end at Sancho's death, when his domains were divided among his sons. The kingdom of Navarre retreated into the Pyrenees as most of its new kings allied themselves with the French and lost interest in Iberian politics. Such was not the case with Ferdinand, the most prominent of Sancho's sons. In the absence of any male heirs to the house of León, he acquired León in 1037.

Ferdinand I went on to conquer the Muslim section of Galicia in what is today northern Portugal. Having added the northern peninsula to his domain, he proclaimed himself emperor of Spain in 1056. It is Ferdinand who is historically credited with beginning the *Reconquista,* the period of reconquest from the Iberian Muslims.

León and Castile would remain undivided until 1157, when León would again become independent. Ferdinand III, king of Castile, finally inherited León in 1230, permanently uniting the two kingdoms. Comprising one of the two great kingdoms of Spain for two centuries, it included Asturias, Córdoba, Estremadura, Galicia, Jaén, and Seville.

The stereotypical notion of today's Spaniard originated in this era of Castilian domination. From the dry plateau in the middle of the peninsula that formed its kingdom in the Middle Ages, Castile succeeded in imposing its style and language on the whole of Spain. The Castilian language became standard Spanish. The name comes from the many castles built to defend the great plains against invaders. The aridity of those plains, the hot wind of summer and the brutal cold of winter, forged a hardened and proud people prepared to go to extremes.

They shared the Iberian Peninsula, as they do today, with four other peoples. The mountainous west on the Atlantic coast

Alfonso II the Chaste ❯
(Alfonsus Castus) of Asturias
adoring Christ, on a
twelfth-century miniature

ADEFONS REX CASTVS

ARMIGER REGIS

1235

TEODEMIRO EPISKOP

Theodomiro, the first bishop of Santiago de Compostela in northern Spain, worshiping the remains of the apostle James, whose body, according to legend, miraculously was brought to Santiago to be buried. The tomb of the apostle is said to have been discovered during Theodomiro's reign.

was inhabited by the Portuguese and the Galicians, who spoke a language closely linked to that of Portugal. To the north lived the Basques, a proud people with a unique language.

To the east of the peninsula, the kingdom of Aragon was inhabited by the Catalans, who spoke a language closely related to the Provençal tongue of the south of France. The Catalans were more adventurous than the restrained farmers of Castile. They took control of Barcelona, Valencia, and the Balearic Islands. Catalan mercenaries and their political leaders would eventually emerge victors in the power struggle in the Mediterranean, even as far away as the Aegean Sea. The king of Aragon, vying with Castile and León for all of Spain, would subdue Sicily, Naples, and Sardinia.

Despite the ethnic and linguistic diversi-

ty of the Iberian peoples, political unity among them steadily increased throughout the Middle Ages. Its peak was to come in 1469 with the marriage between Ferdinand of Aragon and Isabel of Castile. This began the making of Spain as a great power. Ferdinand and Isabel became joint rulers of Castile in 1474 and of Aragon in 1479, but the two kingdoms did not actually unite. King and queen each exercised sovereign power only in his or her own original realm. Castile, by far the wealthier and more populous, dominated not only Aragon, but the Galicians, the Catalans, and the Basques. The desire of all of these for regional autonomy and the free development of their own languages and cultures still continues.

It was under the regency of Ferdinand and Isabel that the Inquisition was established in 1478, allegedly to assure pure faith on the part of Spanish subjects. It also served to reinforce the power of the "Catholic Kings," as they now were called. Royal investigators ("Inquisitors") served both monarchs and church, assisted by informants, condemning anyone they wished in secret proceedings. Royalty, inquisitors, and accusers shared the take, the confiscated property of the victims.

Only the Portuguese escaped the drive toward unification. Conquered by the Muslims in the eighth century, it was partly retaken in 997 by Bermudo II, king of León. Ferdinand I completed the job in 1064 and made fiefs of the reconquered districts. The name Portugal comes from the northern fief, the Comitatus Portaculenis. Some thirty years later, the Muslims invaded Castile. Henry of Burgundy helped Alfonso I of Castile deter them and was, in return, made count of Portugal. After Alfonso died, Henry, and later his widow Teresa, refused allegiance to León. In 1128 his son, Alfonso Henriques (accepted by the nobility as Alfonso I, king of Portugal in 1143), rebelled against Teresa. The pope recognized Portugal as independent in 1179 and encouraged his extension of the kingdom into Muslim regions. Alfonso went as far south as the Tagus River. His son Sancho I, who ruled from 1185 to 1211, settled occupied areas with Christians. The Almohads intervened in this until they were defeated at Navas de Tolosa in Castile in 1212.

The city walls of Marrakech in present-day Morocco. Marrakech was the capital city of the Almohads.

Alfonso III, reigning from 1248 to 1279, finally expelled the last of the Muslims from Portugal and relocated the capital from Coimbra to Lisbon.

Reconquista

The spirit of the reconquista was personified in El Cid (called *El Cid Campeador,* The Lord Champion). Born Rodrigo Díaz de Vivar, he was the son of an unimportant nobleman. Raised with King Sancho II of Castile, he became the king's principal

Section of the embroidered standard of a Muslim army

1237

The Arabs adopted the cultural heritage of the places their conquests took them, adding their own contributions to it. For example, they translated many Greek medical works that otherwise would have been lost forever. This manuscript shows the famous Arab doctor al-Hakim in the company of Hippocrates, Plato, and Aristotle.

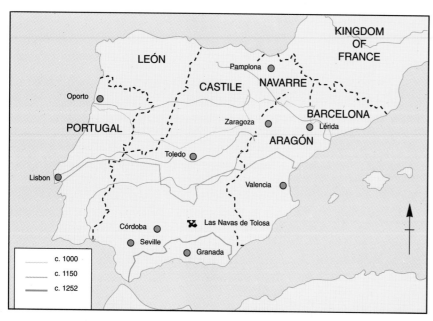

The Christian West waged war with Islam in southern and eastern Europe. This map shows the progress of the Christian armies in their reconquest of Spain.

knight, renowned for his bravery against Aragon for the control of Zaragoza. When Sancho was assassinated, he joined the army of the new king, Alfonso VI. Probably because of his interest in claim-

ing booty as well as victory, he was exiled by Alfonso in 1081. A soldier of fortune, he promptly enlisted in the opposition army and continued his heroic acts, this time with the support of the Muslim *hagibs* (top officials) and the Muslim king of Zaragoza. Eventually reconciled with the king of Castile, he conquered Valencia in 1094, ruling it until his death on July 10, 1099. His deeds are celebrated in numerous ballads; in Spain's most famous epic, *El cantar de mío Cid (The Song of the Cid),* written about 1200; in the twelfth-century Latin *Historia Roderici (History of Rodrigo)*; and in the works of the great Spanish dramatist Lope de Vega.

The reconquest of the Iberian Peninsula begun in 1056 by Ferdinand I did not go evenly. Castile had notable success in the first decades, primarily due to the hopeless disarray of the Muslims after the collapse of their caliphate in Córdoba. Established in the eighth century, it disintegrated in the eleventh into the mutually antagonistic kingdoms of Córdoba, Granada, Lisbon,

Zaragoza, Seville, Murcia, Valencia, and Toledo. Much of the Christian gain was reversed by the arrival of the Muslim sects, the Almoravids and the Almohads, from North Africa. Not until the Christians joined forces at the start of the thirteenth century was the safe continuity of their states assured.

In 1212, while El Cid still ruled Valencia, the Christian kings of Castile and Aragon jointly conquered the city of Toledo. The Castilian king led the onslaught himself and subsequently took up residence there. The most powerful of the remaining Muslims, the Almohads, were soon ousted from Spain by the united Christian front. Several decades later, Aragon would conquer the rich city of Zaragoza. Only a few Muslim enclaves around the port of Cádiz and in Granada survived the purge.

By the fall of Toledo, the reconquista had long ceased to be a matter solely for the resident Christians of Iberia. The reform movement of the Latin church had already come out in support of the concept, the pope had given the campaign his blessing, and the influential Cluny order had already established several supportive monasteries in Spain. Fortune hunters from all over Christendom were likewise encouraged to defend the faith in Spain. They arrived in great numbers, eager to win estates on former Muslim territory, in the name of God. On the no-longer-isolated plains of Castile, the mentality was born that would inspire the later Christian crusaders: a singular mixture of self-interest and religious fervor that would mightily infuse their campaigns.

Italy

Byzantine presence in Italy was briefly established in 535 when Justinian I, emperor of the Eastern Roman Empire, sent Belisarius to oust Germanic invaders. In 572, the Lombards, another Germanic tribe, invaded, eventually reducing Byzantine control to southern Italy and Ravenna in the north. They would remain until the

After the Christian Reconquista of Spain from the Muslims, it took years to erase the predominanat Moorish influence on culture. It is still evident in the architecture of ruins like this hammam (bathhouse) in Ronda, Spain.

The monastery of San Pedro at Cardeña, Spain. The tomb of the legendary El Cid, hero of the Reconquista, is located in the monastery's church.

Franks under Pépin the Short and his son, Charlemagne, intervened at the invitation of the pope in 754, deposing the last Lombard king in 774. Southern Italy became a hodgepodge of small autonomous kingdoms and leftover Byzantine strongholds.

In the ninth century, Muslim invaders appeared, called Saracens by the Christians. (The original Saracens, from the Greek *Sarakenoi*, were tribal people from northern Arabia. The name was used in the Middle Ages for all Arab and Islamic people. The Muslims of northwest Africa who conquered Spain were more often termed Moors.) They drove the remnants of Byzantine authority out of Sicily in 827, establishing several conspicuous bases on the south coast of Italy, and threatening Rome itself.

Pope Leo IV asked the great-grandson of Charlemagne, King Louis II, to help. Louis stopped the Muslims for a time but after he died, they took over the island and southern Italy, compelling the popes to pay them tribute. A period of anarchy ensued as a number of minor kings competed for power. It ended in the north only in 962 when Otto I, who had gained control of both northern Italy and the Lombard realm, was crowned emperor by Pope John XII.

In the south of Italy, however, the Byzantines returned in force in the tenth century. They restored the rule of the

Palermo became a multicultural center after the Muslim conquest of Sicily. On this miniature from c. 1200 depicting the chancellary of Palermo, not only Arabian, but also Greek and Byzantine clerks can be seen.

Basileus (as the emperor in Byzantium was called) in Apulia and Calabria and made the governor of Bari an obedient and effective instrument of their power. The rest of southern Italy remained under Lombard sway.

Around the year 1000, the Muslims were completely driven out of southern Italy. They had to content themselves with the island of Sicily, more easily defended. By then they had made Sicily a magnificent center of Islamic culture. The capital city, Palermo, could almost compete with Cairo and Córdoba.

Normans

At the start of the eleventh century, Pope Benedict VIII granted an audience to several Norman noblemen searching for new opportunities, perhaps even a new homeland. The Holy Father directed them to southern Italy.

In increasingly large numbers, the Normans arrived to seek their fortunes on the Italian coasts. Depending on circumstances, they fought Muslims, Byzantines,

Cloister of Monreale Cathedral, founded near Palermo by the Normans in the twelfth century. The architecture clearly shows both Muslim and Byzantine Christian elements.

1241

and each other, hiring themselves out to local rulers or operating independently. The sons of a certain Tancred de Hauteville were the most successful, seizing Apulia from Byzantine control.

About 1050, another of Tancred's sons,

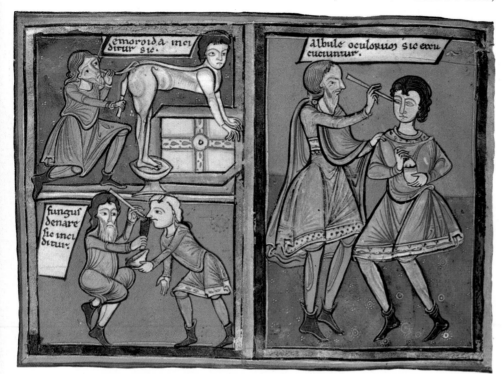

Because of its location, Salerno, Italy, became a melting pot of classical and Arab cultures. Its medical school is considered the precursor of the large medical faculties at the universities of Bologna, Padua, Paris, and Oxford. This twelfth-century miniature depicts several surgical operations.

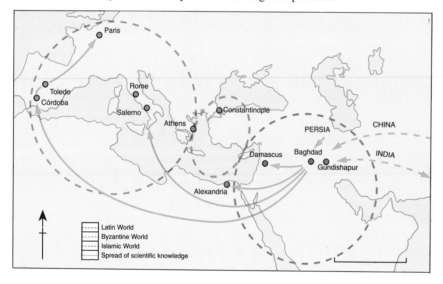

After the fall of the Roman Empire, only fragments of classical literature and science remained in Europe. It was the Islamic world that actually preserved and expanded that knowledge, restoring it to Europe through conquest.

Robert, arrived in Italy. His activities soon won him the epithet *Guiscard*, the cunning one. He began his career as a sheep thief and ended it as ruler of all southern Italy. His skill was evident in his diplomatic approach to the pope, embroiled in conflict with the Holy Roman emperor. Robert realized that he had to legitimize his conquests. In return for an oath of allegiance, he managed to get the pope to grant him

the title of duke. As a papal vassal, he was given not only Apulia and Calabria, but also Sicily, provided he could take it from the Muslims.

In 1061, Robert saw that he had little chance of success himself and sent his brother Roger. It would take thirty years to drive the enemy from the island. Robert rewarded his brother with the title Count of Sicily. The conqueror took residence in Palermo.

Over those decades, Robert Guiscard consolidated his power in southern Italy, taking the Byzantine administrative center of Bari.

After his death, Roger I united southern Italy and Sicily. He created a hybrid central government, supplementing a feudal basis with whatever institutions from previous reigns could reinforce his own position. The Normans succeeding him maintained the administrative system and the customary law of each of the peoples, Roman Catholics, Muslims, and Byzantine Greeks, under their control on condition that each group recognize the authority of the ruler of Palermo.

The resulting state attained a level of development and prosperity unmatched in the Christian world. It seemed a fusing of Christian and Islamic culture was possible under the Norman dukes. The ruler, living as an emir complete with harem, appeared to synthesize the faiths of pope and caliph. In 1127, Roger II, count of Sicily, was recognized as duke of Apulia and Calabria. In 1130, when he assumed the title of king of Sicily, he may not have been the most powerful, but he was certainly the wealthiest king in all Christendom. He also had the most loyal subjects. His domain was sometimes called the Kingdom of the Two Sicilies because the southern part of the Italian mainland was known as "Sicily on this side of Cape Faro." It was not until the thirteenth century that the Norman Empire would become caught up in the great dynastic conflicts that would lead to its downfall, a drama that would involve all of Europe.

The creation of that empire demonstrated clearly that the Muslims were far from invincible. Their dominance of the Mediterranean was also under attack. In the north Italian commercial towns of Genoa and Pisa, flotillas were built to challenge the notorious Islamic captains in their own element. They scored victory after victory. Sardinia and Corsica, long under Muslim supremacy, were captured. The Muslims even lost the Balearic Islands.

View of the south facade of the Hagia Sophia (also known as St. Sophia), the Church of Holy Wisdom, in Istanbul. Construction began in 532 by order of Emperor Justinian. The minarets were built in the Ottoman era, after the church was converted into a mosque.

Byzantium

The Christian Stronghold in the East

The western part of the Roman Empire broke up in the fifth century AD. The eastern part (or the Byzantine Empire, after the ancient name of the capital, Byzantium) existed from 330 to 1453. The Byzantines melded Roman legal and administrative institutions, orthodox Christian religion, and Greek language into a single unsurpassed culture. Its emperors regarded the former Roman borders as their own.

Over the fifth and sixth centuries, there were repeated incursions by Germanic and Hunnic tribes. Between 534 and 565, the emperor Justinian I, aided by his wife Theodora, tried to restore both the cultural and the territorial greatness of the Roman Empire, retaking North Africa, Italy, some of Spain, and the Mediterranean islands of Sicily and Sardinia.

At its peak about 550, the empire almost encircled the Mediterranean, encompassing its islands and parts of southern Spain, Italy, southeastern Europe, the Balkan

A farmer using oxen as draught animals to plow his land; from an eleventh-century Byzantine manuscript

Two of these coins depict Emperor Justinian II, while the third (*bottom*) coin shows a portrait of Christ.

Peninsula, southwestern Asia, Palestine, Egypt, and northeastern Africa.

Later the same century, the Byzantines lost most of northern Italy (outside Rome, Ravenna, and Naples) to the Lombards and most of the Balkans to Turkish Avar cavalry and the Slavic tribes who moved in after them to claim abandoned villages. The Byzantine grip on the Mediterranean region had begun to weaken.

The seventh century was the low point. The assassination of Mauricius, the first Byzantine emperor to be murdered, initiated a period of great civil strife. Christian sects vied for control, undermining popular confidence in government. In 610, Heraclius (circa 575-641) overthrew the emperor Phocas who had been in power only since 602. Mongolian Avars and Persians promptly invaded. In 622, Heraclius counterattacked, driving the Persians from Asia Minor, Egypt, and Syria and invading Persia in 628. Over the next two years, he recovered the Christian relic called the True Cross from the Persians and sent the Avars back to central Europe. Yet he lost them all to the Arabs again (and Mesopotamia, as well) between 634 and 642.

Greek Influence

Even in the seventh century, despite the predominant Greek influence, the emperors still addressed their subjects as *Romaioi* (Romans). Foreigners called them *Graeci* (Greeks) because Greek was their mother tongue. Greek was a highly developed language, with a rich and varied literature. It was used for all administrative, legal, scientific, and educational purposes, although some subjects spoke Coptic, Syriac, Armenian, and other local dialects. Latin was no longer in much active use, even at court.

Absolute Power

The emperor himself was no longer titled *caesar* or *imperator* (emperor). He was called by the purely Greek word *basileus*, meaning king or emperor. The source of all secular law and governmental authority, he also played a vital part in religious matters. The basileus was expected to lend imperial authority to a single church doctrine. He

had the final decision in selecting the head of the church, the patriarch of Constantinople, as well as all political and military appointments.

The church, an instrument in the hands of the court, emphasized the divine nature of imperial power, viewing it as granted by God. This principle had been established by Constantine. The basileus was seen as God's representative on Earth, not sacred in and of himself but occupying an imperial throne that it was sinful to resist. This

This page from a tenth-century Byzantine manuscript depicts tableaus of life in the countryside: a shepherd playing his flute while tending the cattle, the farmer taking care of his crop, and a fisherman.

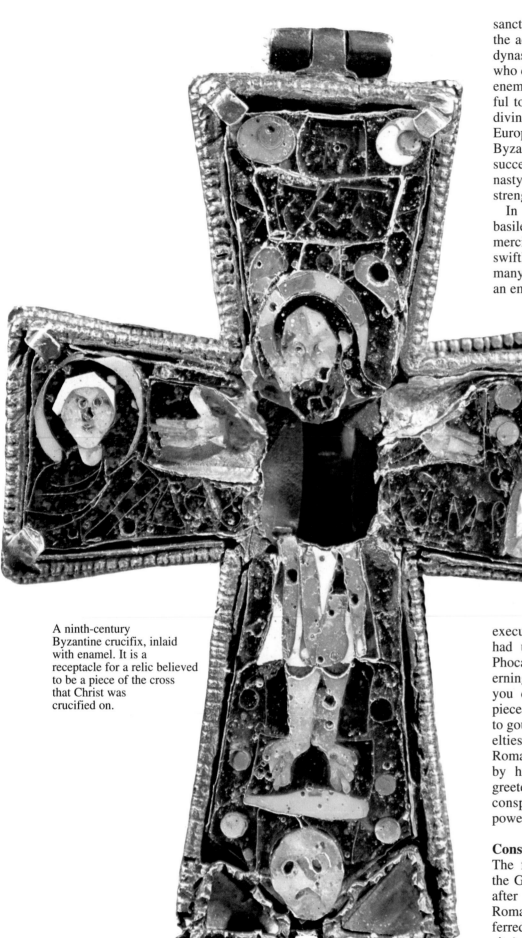

A ninth-century Byzantine crucifix, inlaid with enamel. It is a receptacle for a relic believed to be a piece of the cross that Christ was crucified on.

sanctity of the institution did not extend to the actual person of the emperor or to his dynasty. These were just human beings who could be sinners themselves, potential enemies of God. It was not regarded as sinful to cause their downfall. The notion of divine right to rule as conceived of in Europe centuries later was unknown in the Byzantine Empire. There was no law of succession to the throne. If a particular dynasty continued, it did so because of the strength of that imperial family.

In fact, it was dangerous to harm the basileus in any way. He was surrounded by merciless political groups who responded swiftly to rumors of treason. The careers of many a civil servant and soldier, and even an emperor, were ended by the hand of the executioner. (As example, when Heraclius had usurped the power of the emperor Phocas, he asked, "Do you call that governing?" Phocas replied: "Do you think you can do better?" He was hacked to pieces then and there.) A later practice was to gouge out an opponent's eyes. Such cruelties were not the rule. The emperor Romanus was put in a remote monastery by his rebellious sons, whom he later greeted as fellow inmates when a new conspiracy brought another relative to power.

Constantinople: The Great Splendor

The first Christian emperor, Constantine the Great, renamed the city of Byzantium after himself and made it a capital of the Roman Empire in 330. The Vikings referred to Constantinople as *Mikligardr* (big city) and respectfully called the Bosporus the *Sjavidarsund* (Straits of the Devout Believers).

Throughout their reign, the Byzantines regarded their capital as the center of the world. They were contemptuous of barbaric westerners, with their rough language and peasant clothing. This was understandable given the magnificence of the Church of Aya Sofia, the Grand Palace glittering in the sun, and the emperor bedecked with jewels. The majestic God, they felt, had chosen Constantinople to be the center of His Church, His Truth, and His Empire.

The basileus kept court at Constantine's palace on the Bosporus Straits. The city stretched for miles around it. All roads, all administrative channels came together in Constantinople. The metropolis was so immense and so important in comparison to the provinces that the possession of it meant the possession of the empire. Constantinople withstood major Arab sieges in the 670s and again in 717 and 718. Beseiging rioters and raiders faced with its unscalable walls soon realized that they had won nothing without the city, yet often a well-organized internal coup was enough to take power. Any basileus withstanding a siege retained his power intact. The administrative effort was on keeping the people of the capital happy.

Civil Service

The emperor was responsible for the civil service, notable for its attention to matters of protocol. Most of his servants had one thing in common: they had risen through the ranks by diligence and cunning. Hardly ever descended from old aristocratic families, they were created by the empire (per-

This depiction of Christ on the cross, lamented by his mother and John, is a section of the cover of a Byzantine manuscript, richly decorated with gold and precious stones.

A mosaic from the Imperial Palace, Constantinople, sixth century. This shows the fine quality of mosaic artists continuing the antique style.

ο σαρι αρχ και σε κ αλε μπει· παρα αμα χι μα απο λαβειν το ρ αα σαα σαμαν τας εικονας· και α πακλη σι μ γενεας

Της αλσε βειασ + ο πρι αρχ και νδεσ αποστελα φ μπρ ρ σμασιλεω

μιστορο ζα φορ σι τουρμαν· πτ σ σκουσ αγαλ μησ τ αοσι·

ο βασιλεω σμι ος σα μσο τ σμαν

ν αι νι αι σ επ σι και νεπα· ιων πτ ν α και ουα σι αν σ υ σ φτι ι π σ ιω πσ ο μ αι σσι σ· μ μ πτ μ μ ν πτ ι υ η σ τμ σαραδδ νο

A Byzantine emperor receiving a delegation at the court; thirteenth-century miniature

sonified in the basileus) and were completely dependent on it. Loyalty to imperial institutions was their only guarantee to a good life. Few tried to undermine those structures for any reason. In general, civil servants were well educated. They knew their classics, were well informed about the main issues of theology, and were quite familiar with the highly complicated forms of Byzantine etiquette. Most were recruited by the basileus from the parts of the city just outside its great entry point, the Bronze Gate. They came from a different social class than the military commanders recruited from the provinces, often from outlying districts like Armenia. The two groups (civil service and military) hated each other.

The Army

After a chaotic period of rapid imperial succession, civil authority over newly organized provinces (called *themes*) fell to the Byzantine military commanders successful in the constant border wars. The emperor Heraclius is credited with establishing the new theme system, a complex military apparatus with a hierarchy of functionaries to provide administration.

The army was made over into an elite guard (the *tagmata*) and an army corps, the *themata* (or themes). Each was commanded by a *stratégos* (or general) with both civil and military authority over regional military districts. Officers had to be able to speak two languages in addition to the Greek, dominant only in the capital, in order to communicate with the soldiers.

The Byzantine army was large and varied in language and ethnic background. The core consisted of professional regiments with well-motivated soldiers who were excellent fighters, but the great mass of soldiers were unwilling draftees who were forced to serve and had trouble figuring out why. Thematic army soldiers were given tax-exempt land in lieu of cash. This at once rewarded them, retained land within the empire, and avoided the cash drain previously incurred by salaried armies in the past.

The Economy

Justinian's sixth-century conquests, in particular, had been costly to the empire. In his effort to restore old grandeur, he had also erected expensive public buildings and churches. Conquest and construction alike emptied imperial coffers. The plague, meanwhile, filled coffins. A century later, the negative impact of war and civil disorder on agriculture, trade, and the quality of urban life was evident. The empire lacked the resources to maintain its prior glory.

A number of solutions were found. Since hunger lay at the root of most civil discontent and rebellion, the basileus saw to it that there was always enough food for the eight hundred thousand inhabitants of the capital. Enormous warehouses stored an abundance of grain to guarantee supplies even after bad harvests.

In addition, strict price controls insured that almost everyone could buy food at reasonable prices. Even the lowest-paid day laborer earned enough to feed his family. The really poor were not abandoned. Belief in charity was central to the eastern church and all kinds of high-ranking people, led by the emperor, tried to prove they practiced it. Huge public handouts of fish and bread regularly took place in the hippodrome. Funerals were frequently viewed as occasions for providing food to the poor.

There was no starvation in the city as the result of the high subsidies and handouts, but the economy was paralyzed by scores of regulations. The emperors did not allow high wages. The average Byzantine was hopelessly underpaid and had to compete for work with the free labor of the flood of slaves captured by the imperial army on its successful campaigns. (Remarkably enough, the position of day laborers improved with the large military defeats of the eleventh century. The supply of slaves dwindled and wages increased accordingly.)

Often, the common man could not even afford clothing, the price of woven cloth was so high. Many people wore rags or improvised some sort of clothing from straw. Given the problems of shelter, inadequate clothing was often fatal. In the winter, violent rainstorms beat down on the streets and icy gales swept in from the Ukraine keeping temperatures around freezing much of the time. Tens of thousands of shivering people found their only shelter in the windy, half-open galleries of the main streets. Constantinople had an enormous housing problem. The rents were high and the rooms were small.

All this was part of an unhealthy economy. The Byzantine Empire was the direct descendant of Diocletian's Edict of 301. As emperor of Rome from 284 to 305, Diocletian reorganized imperial administration and centralized control, setting maximum commodity prices and wages for the entire empire. While that edict proved unenforceable, his changes in tax collecting had lasting impact. Making the collectors themselves responsible for paying the taxes, he created a basis for serfdom.

Taxes

Constantinople was the glutton of the empire. The provinces had to pay for the maintenance of the grand capital and got nothing in return except corrupt civil servants. The villages were taxed annually. After harvesttime, the tax collector would appear with a company of soldiers to get his payment regardless of the quality of the harvest or problems of drought or locusts.

Desperate peasants fled to join the masses in the big city or joined bands of rob-

bers, knowing that their families would have to pay their debts. The provinces grew increasingly poor. Peasants were forced to abandon their farms. Whole villages became depopulated. These conditions provided good opportunities for the

rich, looking for profitable investments. They bought more and more land, eventually owning estates that stretched for miles. Some historians refer to this as the feudalization of the Byzantine Empire, although conditions east and west were quite different.

In contrast to the West with its social

The Byzantines possessed a high level of military knowledge. Fast and agile warships, powered by rowers, were built at the naval shipyard in Constantinople. They could be used as the foundation for a temporary bridge, as seen on this ninth-century miniature. 1249

phenomenon termed feudalism, no oath or contract was established between a landowner and his tenants. Their relationship was purely commercial rather than one of allegial obligation. The new landowners became far more powerful opponents for both church and basileus than the small farmers had been. They developed into an influential class, although the basileus himself was the largest landholder during most of the empire's history.

Monetary System

Constantine established an innovative monetary system with his empire that would last to the eleventh century. Based on the gold coin called the *solidus* or the *nomisma*, it kept the empire together as an economic unit despite the problems of the lower classes. Both the purity and the supply of precious metal were controlled by the government. Commerce and craftsmanship increased. From the fourth through the sixth centuries, there was considerable prosperity everywhere in the empire. Urban economies developed. Agriculture remained overall productive even as the burdensome taxes forced farmers to abandon their land. Large estates began to predominate the society, many held by the church.

The Church

The church remained the most influential factor in society. Every basileus sought religious harmony to placate its powerful officials and to garner the divine favor seen as essential to the very existence of the empire. The overthrow of a basileus often had consequences for the church. The patriarch who headed the Byzantine church, the religious counterpart to the pope in Rome, was usually awarded his position by the basileus. The downfall of the basileus, therefore, usually cost the patriarch his place as well, especially if the new ruler had different religious views.

Theology was the paramount topic of discussion among the Byzantines, who were divided into mutually hostile philosophical camps. As soon as one problem seemed to be resolved, another would appear. Theological battles, some lasting

An eagle, the symbol
of Byzantine power, on a
piece of silk.
Silk was produced in great
quantities in Constantinople.
Only the emperor was
allowed to wear the
purple variant.

for centuries, were fought with hair-splitting subtlety and intense emotional argument, and not only among the elite. Heated biblical discussions took place in all classes of society.

The issue of Monophysitism, for example, was debated throughout the fifth and sixth centuries and has not yet been resolved. A Christian sect primarily within the Eastern Church, the Monophysites maintained that Christ had only one nature, which was divine. This put them in theoretical opposition to the orthodox doctrine that Jesus was at once divine and human. Although the movement had few western advocates, Pope Leo I tried to accommodate it at the Council of Chalcedon in 451. His moderating edict satisfied no one. The argument ran on into the next century, when Byzantium excommunicated the heretical Monophysites. They then formally seceded from the Eastern Church. They refused to recognize the authority of the basileus, especially with regard to tax collection. Many of them left the empire altogether and started paying taxes to the caliph of Baghdad. The sect itself subsequently divided over the question of the incorruptibility of the body of Christ.

Another controversy arose about 560 over the nature of God. Another group, the Tritheists, insisted that the three persons of the Christian deity (Father, Son, and Holy Ghost) were to be considered three separate gods. The only agreement in centuries was reached: everyone outside the Tritheist sect considered them heretics.

Meanwhile, in Mesopotamia, Egypt, and Syria, Monophysitism prospered. Condemned by ecumenical council in 680-681, it continues today in the Coptic, Abyssinian, Armenian, and Jacobite churches.

Byzantine Art and the Worship of Icons

Although Byzantine artists created luxury objects of ivory and enamel for secular use, much of the empire's early art reflected the demands of the church. The focus was on pictorial representation of religious subjects rather than the veneration of actual relics (bits of bone, hair, or clothing) of saints practiced in the West. Techniques of art changed, the very physical modeling of classical Hellenic statuary yielding to the Byzantine emphasis on spirituality. By the fifth century, sculpture was used to carve *diptychs* (ivory plaques) rather than statues. Many of the Byzantine consuls had their portraits done on such ivory diptychs, a matter of concern to the emperor who preferred his to be the only image depicted. The walls of the once-bare basilicas were

covered with religious images in paint and mosaic. *Tesserae* (tiny cubes) of colored glass or stone made up the mosaics. Sometimes overlaid with gold leaf (very thin sheets of hammered gold), they offered an exquisite beauty appropriate to the magnificence of both God and empire, and contributed to the "other worldly" atmosphere in the churches.

Byzantine art and architecture flourished during the reign of their patron emperor Justinian (527-565). The finest mosaics of his era are still to be found on the walls of the Church of San Vitale, in Ravenna, Italy. Completed in 547, they mingle Old Testament scenes with Christian imagery.

Jesus Christ, without a beard, is seated on the globe of the world, shown with his earthly representative, the emperor Justinian, and the empress Theodora, together with their attendants.

Over a five-year period, Justinian had the *Hagia Sophia*, or the Church of the Holy Wisdom, erected in Constantinople. Consecrated in 537, it is a great dome 185 feet high set above a huge square formed, in turn, by four arches. Created by the architects Anthemius of Tralles and Isidorus of Miletus, it constitutes a major innovation in architecture through its use of four curved triangles, called pendentives, to provide transitional support between the circular dome and its square

In Greece, Byzantine monks built twenty-four monasteries in high mountainous locations, beginning in the fourteenth century. Collectively referred to as *Meteora* (poised between heaven and earth), these monasteries were strictly ascetic.

Romanian culture also experienced Byzantine influence. The fifteenth-century monastery church of Voronet in Romania, shown here, was built in a style that combines Gothic and Byzantine elements. The inner and outer walls are painted with frescoes of scenes from both Romanian folklore and the Bible.

base. Like all other Byzantine churches, the outside is plain. It is the interior artwork that counted.

People worshiped that art as symbolic of God. Icons in the churches were usually flat portraits of Christ and the saints done in oil paint, mosaic, gold, or ivory. The theological argument had to do with the concept of the incarnation, the basic Christian belief that God was present in the man Jesus. The fact that Jesus was born a human allowed for the belief that artistic representations of him, both painted images and carved icons, somehow shared in his divinity. To reject that possibility, believers in icons contended, was to reject the possibility of the incarnation, as well. Icons were believed to provide direct personal contact with Christ or the saints depicted on them. They could be objects of *proskynesis* (veneration) but not *latreia* (worship), which was reserved for God. Outside the churches, small paintings done on wood were available and affordable to the common man and seen as beneficial in the home. People buying them were

considered devout. Some icons were thought to have healing power.

Iconoclasm

Some members of the Eastern Church had always objected to portraying religious scenes and people. Church fathers, both east and west, had objected to the practice, pointing to the biblical prohibition against the worship of graven images. Most notable among them was Saint Augustine, bishop of Hippo (in North Africa) in 395. A latecomer to Christianity, Augustine would become the most prominent theologian in Roman Catholicism. The use of icons was still controversial three centuries after his death.

Coming from the Greek words *eikon* (image) and *kloein* (break), iconoclasm defines a philosophy opposed to the religious use of icons. Iconoclasts called their opponents *ikonodouloi* (or servants of images).

The movement had a counterpart in the Muslim countries of the Umayyad caliphate. In 723, the caliph Yazid issued

an edict banning the making of religious images. Given that their worship is forbidden by the Islamic scripture, the Koran, the fact that a caliph objected to icons was not surprising. What made Yazid take action, according to legend, was a visit he had on his deathbed from a Jewish visitor named *Tessarakontapechys* (meaning "forty elbows," or Visir, for short). He predicted that the caliph would live to a ripe old age if he destroyed all the icons in his empire. The caliph recovered and had the images removed from all the churches in his kingdom. Perhaps he had simply been persuaded by Jewish civil servants that iconoclasm was necessary.

The Byzantine Empire had good trade relations with the Russian principality of Kiev. This resulted in extensive Byzantine influence and the conversion of the Russians to Christianity in 984. The first Christian churches, like this one in Suzdal, were built of wood.

Three years later, the first iconoclast order was issued in Constantinople by Emperor Leo III. His command to destroy all icons came soon after a major natural disaster, which may have influenced it. In 726, the sea began to boil one day near the island of Thera. Clouds of steam obscured the sun, lava spewed from the water, and a tidal wave ravaged the nearby coasts. A new island rose from the Aegean Sea. People no doubt wondered if it was a sign from God.

Gold cover of a tenth-century Byzantine evangelistary, showing Jesus Christ, the apostles, archangels, and others

The emperor subsequently had the icon of Christ by the Bronze Gate demolished. He had been converted to iconoclasm. The destruction of that icon at the entrance to his palace was the start of a campaign to destroy not only icons, but all representation of the human figure in religious art. Everywhere but Italy, which refused to comply, religious images were smashed to pieces by the authorities, yet nothing was heard from him. Officially, Leo was silent about his conversion. It was not until 730, four years later, that he issued an edict from the throne hall prohibiting the veneration of icons.

The emperor could boast impressive military success. In 717, he had deposed Emperor Theodosius III and successfully withstood the siege of Constantinople. He had brought the Muslim attacks to a halt with his reorganized defenses and his "Greek fire," a highly flammable secret mixture of saltpeter and naphtha. He had brought the empire back from the edge of anarchy. Thunder and lightning, pestilence, and earthquakes held off after his edict, so that even God himself, or so many of the Byzantine people thought, supported the new ideas.

The announcement was condemned by the pope in Rome. Most lay Latin Christians simply could not accept the destruction, although few understood the precise reasons for it. Some Byzantine intellectuals had doubts about the new movement, as well. The iconodules used the angry letters from the pope to point to the authority that the Holy See had over the entire church. The iconoclasts insisted on the special position of the Eastern Church and its patriarch. The basileus himself resisted the influence of the pope in his empire for reasons not altogether religious: he had always wanted to bring the whole hierarchy under his power.

The Monasteries

Leo III died in 741. Under his son and successor Constantine V, reinforcement of iconoclasm continued rigorously. In 754, at a church council held at his summer palace in Hieria, Constantine V had image worship condemned as idolatry. There was a lot of resistance from the monasteries, strongholds of the iconodules. Any clergyman caught venerating an icon had it smashed to pieces on his head. Iconodules were frequently persecuted, forced to marry, some even tortured to death. This created a number of icon-defending heroes and martyrs. Constantine confiscated their property.

Latin Christianity regarded the iconoclastic movement in the East as scandalous heresy and condemned it in the strongest possible terms. The latent conflict between the Latin and the Greek Christians became more and more intense. Certainly religious in nature, the controversy is considered by some modern historians to be sociological in origin. They claim a class distinction between the adherents of the opposing views, contending that iconodules tended to be prosperous landowners and civil servants, while iconoclasts were among the less privileged.

Interior of a Byzantine church in Cappadocia that was hewed from the rocks. Such churches served as refuges during invasions by Arabs and other enemies.

The Middle Byzantine Empire

Still the Center of the World

The Byzantine basileus (emperor) Leo III, the Isaurean, ruled from 717 to 741 with lasting impact. He issued the historic ban on the veneration of icons that set off public explosion of the long-running theological argument over iconoclasm. It would not be resolved for a century. He also issued a modified legal code, the *Ecloga*, in 739. It would be used for the next two hundred years. Considered the man who saved the Eastern Empire from certain chaos, he founded the Isaurean dynasty. That lasted until 802, to the regret of those under its final empress.

The Byzantine imperial policy remained iconoclastic after Leo's death, but the climate under his heirs grew increasingly more agreeable for those venerating icons. Leo the Isaurean's grandson, Emperor Leo IV, married a girl from minor Athenian aristocracy in 769. Irene was beautiful and intelligent, as the regulations on imperial

Valuable Byzantine reliquary shaped like a church

marriages required, but she was an iconodule, regarding icons as a means to religious experience. Despite the official edicts against it, her husband had no objection. In the beginning, she stayed in the background. Leo IV died in 780, some years after his coronation. He left an underage son, Constantine VI, and a throne vacant for the time being. His widow hungered for the throne.

The Merciless Irene

Irene succeeded in securing the regency for herself, nominally ruling on behalf of her son. She gradually managed to alter the government policy on icons, restoring the practice outlawed by Leo III and his son Constantine V.

Council of Nicaea: 787

In 787, Irene summoned the second Council of Nicaea to condemn iconoclasm. It did so. The decision and the fact that the regent had taken a hand in religious affairs aroused great popular hostility. The people were already dissatisfied with her penchant for power and her obsession with the icon-venerating cause.

The young Constantine presented an obstacle. In an effort to prevent him from becoming emperor, Irene had him put in prison. The move was not well considered. She suddenly found herself with no support. The *Armeniakoi*, an Armenian regiment of great military and political importance, mutinied in protest. Constantine VI was crowned emperor. Irene and the coterie of eunuchs who advised her faded from the scene for a time.

Two years later, the new basileus had

Coin with the portrait of Emperor Leo III. The iconoclasm movement began during his reign (717-741).

1256

succeeded in making enemies of his followers. The radical iconodules were particularly distressed by the fact that he divorced his first wife and married another. Irene was called back to the court with much publicity and fanfare. Behind the scenes, she reassembled her supporters, laying the groundwork for a new government and plotting to undermine her son. While he was off on a military campaign, she seized power. Constantine VI, lacking any backers of his own, was returned to the capital city. His mother then ordered his eyes gouged out. Six weeks later, Constantine VI died. The news and the manner of his death were received with horror across the empire.

The pitiless Irene did nothing to improve her reputation. Rather than following the tradition of choosing a husband to rule, she had herself crowned empress and began to wear the ceremonial robes of the basileus. In the West, the Byzantine throne was considered vacant after the death of Constantine VI: No woman could be basileus.

Despite the decision at the Council of Nicaea, the iconoclasm controversy continued to divide the empire east and west. The pope sought alliance elsewhere. On Christmas Day in 800, he crowned the Frank Charlemagne emperor of the Holy Roman Empire.

Constantinople was rocked. Government in the Eastern Empire was already paralyzed by constant struggle among the powerful eunuchs of the imperial retinue. Irene tried to recover her popularity by dramatically reducing taxes. This unsettled the Byzantine economy and cost the empress the confidence of the court.

Under the leadership of Nicephorus, the minister of finance, Irene lost her throne in a bloodless palace revolution in 802. When she persisted in conspiring to get it back, Nicephorus had her put in a nunnery. She died within the year, the last of the Isaurean dynasty.

Brief Reigns: Nicephorus, Stauracius, and Michael I

Nicephorus did his best to repair the economic and political damage. He instituted diplomatic relations with Charlemagne, put the imperial finances in order, and organized military campaigns against the pagan Bulgarians invading from the north. He was killed in battle against them.

His son Stauracius, wounded seriously on the same occasion, tried to govern from bed. Stauracius, in turn, became the victim of a palace revolution that brought

his brother-in-law Michael to the throne for want of someone better. Now called Michael I, the new basileus was an icon venerator who tried to govern in the middle of growing iconoclastic upheavals. The army had long ago lost confidence in iconodule rulers and prayed for the resurrection of iconoclast Constantine V.

Their officers, more prone to direct action, led the basileus into a Bulgarian ambush. He survived but it gave Leo V, the Armenian military leader of the Armeniakoi, reason to overthrow the government and its military. Michael voluntarily surrendered to the usurper and was locked up in a monastery.

The monastery of Hosios Lucas (St. Luke), one of the best-preserved Byzantine monasteries in Greece, built in the early eleventh century

Exterior view of the rock church of St. Barbara in Göreme, Cappadocia, erected at the peak of the iconoclasm movement

Section of the interior of St. Barbara. Iconoclasm accounts for the striking difference between this church and the one shown on page 1255.

Armenians on the Throne

Leo the Armenian, a moderate iconoclast, restored the economy and the military might of the Byzantine Empire, but petty palace intrigue prevailed. His own aide, Michael, was arrested on Christmas night in 820 on a charge of high treason. Michael was put in chains, to be executed after Christmas, but with the help of his guard he managed to get word to his fellow conspirators. On the following morning, disguised as monks, they got into the palace chapel and killed Leo. In great haste, they put Michael, with the chains still around his feet, on the throne and crowned him

A priest being flogged during the reign of Michael II (820-829). Miniature from a Byzantine chronicle

emperor. Because they continued to retain ties with the Armeniakoi, he and his immediate successors were referred to as Armenians.

Michael II was hardly secure. In Asia Minor, a rebellion had begun under the leadership of Thomas the Slav, once a fellow officer and friend of the new basileus and his predecessor. Thomas was on good terms with the discontented segments of society. He recruited a huge army of dissatisfied farmers and adventurers and, with Muslim support, laid siege to the capital. A Bulgarian attack broke them. Thomas was captured and killed.

Council of Orthodoxy: 843

Over the ninth century, the Byzantine Empire made a strong recovery. Muslim attacks halted as Byzantine power grew and that of the caliphate faded. In the reign of Michael's son Theophilus, Constantinople glittered as never before. Although he fought border wars against the caliph, Theophilus admired Islamic culture. He collected art and had his palace decorated in lavish Arabic style. His wife Theodora took the view that artistic representation of the sacred was acceptable. The gentle iconoclast Theophilus offered no objection. When Theophilus died, she took over the government on behalf of their three-year-old son Michael III. In 843, Empress Theodora II convened the Council of Orthodoxy. It restored the veneration of icons to legitimacy, honoring her request that the name of Theophilus would not be

cursed. This was the final condemnation of iconoclasm.

Like its introduction by the order of Leo III, the condemnation of iconoclasm at the councils in 787 and 843 was, in fact, imperial in origin rather than religious. Both ecclesiastical councils were convened by empresses. Both, although debated and voted on in theological council, carried out the whim of the incumbent empress. In each case, the authority of the imperial throne was reinforced. The secular was determining the spiritual, the state making decisions for the church as to the very nature of its worship.

The Macedonian Dynasty: 867-1056

Michael III, taking on the imperial mantle as an adult, became an alcoholic. In 866, at the age of twenty-six, he appointed his

Tenth-century Byzantine chest made of skillfully decorated ivory panels. The decoration consists of subjects from classical mythology, such as the labors of Hercules.

The dome of the Hagia Sophia in Nicaea, where the great council was convened in 787

chamberlain Basil as coemperor. The action would cost Michael his power and, a year later, his life. Basil had him put to death for delirium.

Basil I (812-886)

The new sole ruler of the empire was born a peasant in Macedonia. His first contact with the man who made him emperor was through his work as a groom in the imperial stables in Constantinople. Ruling from 867 until his death in 886, Basil introduced a number of reforms in the administration of government. He began an overhaul of the legal system eventually completed by his son Leo VI. Byzantine recovery would reach its peak under the Macedonian dynasty he founded. Its name is taken from Basil's birthplace; the dynasty would rule until 1081. His descendants would hold power for nearly two centuries.

Constantine Porphyrogenitus (905-959)

Constantine VII, called Constantine Porphyrogenitus, owes his imperial epithet (the name means "born in purple") to the emperorship of his father. Ascending the throne in 913, he ruled until 959. He had had a lifetime to develop the scholarly

nature for which he is remembered. While his brothers maneuvered for power, Constantine was a patron of scholarship and wrote books himself on various aspects of government. His *De Thematibus* (*On the Provinces*) details the history of some of the Byzantine territories. *De Administrando Imperio* (*On Imperial Administration*) is a manual on how to govern people in the eastern Europe of the time. The subject of *De Ceremoniis Aulae Byzantinae* (*Byzantine Court Ceremonies*) is obvious from its title. The basileus proved highly capable of putting the advice from his own books into practice.

Not only did he run an effective administration, he was also responsible for a cultural renaissance in the empire. He sponsored the recopying of ancient manuscripts, the writing of new reference works, and the revived study of science, mathematics, and literature. Constantine found more pleasure in the law than in war, leaving that to his generals, who were as unschooled as their superior was civilized. They sought to retake the Muslim states of Mesopotamia and Syria.

The literary emperor was dominated by his father-in-law and coemperor, Romanus I, who was ousted from Constantinople in 944. Even then, Constantine continued the efforts to protect small farmers they had begun jointly. He also continued the contact they had established with people in Russia, interested in making Christians of them.

Nicephorus Phocas
The son of Constantine Porphyrogenitus, Romanus II, died after a short reign. His wife Theophano now had the right to give her hand in marriage, and the crown with it, to the man of her choice. The bureaucracy and the army were fiercely in opposition to each other as to the type of husband the empress should choose. The civil servants tried to prevent her marrying a military man. The reconqueror of Crete, the well-known Nicephorus Phocas, who had been

Tenth-century miniature depicting Leo V the Armenian being proclaimed emperor in 813

1261

Eleventh-century
mosaic. Constantine IX
Monomachus
is shown next to
Jesus Christ, who is
making a gesture of blessing
with his right hand.

Constantine's best general, wanted to marry the empress. He represented everything the civilized city-dwellers detested. He was uneducated and behaved like a peasant, was tyrannical and lived like an ascetic, without any luxuries at all. Indisputably, he was an excellent soldier.

Nicephorus marched on to the capital city, married Theophano, and mounted the gilded throne.

Nicephorus was not an unscrupulous careerist. He fought with religious fervor against the Muslims. A Christian crusader, he made no effort to control the looting and pillaging of his soldiers as long as the cause of Christianity was advanced by the violence. The terrified Muslims nicknamed him Pale Death. He put everything in the empire into the service of the military. Every victory meant new attacks, new weapons, new taxes. Constantinople was flooded with soldiers who rioted in the streets and caused trouble to civilians. The crusading emperor fighting for the universal Christ was soon universally detested at home as well as abroad.

The new basileus also antagonized the church by confiscating property from the monasteries. However, when he also demanded that the patriarch declare every soldier killed in the war an officially recognized saint, the church had had enough. In 969, top palace officials organized a conspiracy to get rid of him. The resentful Empress Theophano was involved. With

The Great Schism of 1054

Divisions between Eastern and Western Christianity were evident at least by the fourth century and debated in various ecclesiastical councils for centuries. The two branches of the church grew increasingly far apart over issues of language, liturgy, celibacy, religious art, and church organization. However, it was the question of the location of ultimate church authority that led most directly to the Great Schism, the formal separation of the Eastern Orthodox Church from the Western Roman Catholic Church in 1054.

Byzantine or Orthodox Christianity was a fellowship of independent ("autocephalus") churches run by their own head bishops (called patriarchs) rather than by a hierarchy dominated by a single pope as the Roman church was. The word orthodox, taken from the Greek for "right-believing," is used to designate various branches of Christianity originally in the East, including the church in Byzantium (Constantinople) and the other ancient domains (or patriarchates) in Alexandria, Egypt; Antioch; Jerusalem; and Damascus, Syria, (where Arabic is used in lieu of Greek).

No patriarch claimed authority outside his own region. The patriarch at Constantinople was considered first among equals in a system of church councils. He was not considered infallible. Patriarchal authority, determined by historical factors, was called "pragmatic." Papal authority, in contrast, was considered final in the West; the pope was regarded as infallible.

In the south of Italy, the Latin Normans had conquered the Byzantine Greeks and forced them to give up their eastern liturgy for the Latin counterpart. Michael I Cerularius, patriarch of Constantinople from 1043 to 1057, responded by forcing the Latin Christians who were still under the power of Byzantium to adopt the eastern liturgy. Made patriarch by Basileus Constantine IX three years after he first became a monk, Cerularius had helped overthrow the previous emperor, Michael IV.

In Rome, great consternation and anger followed his action. Major differences were seen in the way the Eucharist or the rite of Communion was carried out. Latins used unleavened bread, for instance, while Greeks did not; Latins repeated the words of Christ while the Greeks invoked more general church prayer. In another major issue, the Roman church required celibacy; the Byzantine did not.

The theologian and papal legate Humbert wrote a fierce defense of the western position. In 1054, he placed a

papal bull on the altar of the Hagia Sofia Church, an official document excommunicating Michael and the whole Eastern church. The basileus responded by objecting to the papal doctrine of supremacy. He convened a synod, a meeting of all orthodox clergy, which denied the pope any further say in the affairs of the Eastern church, excommunicating him in turn. The synod's encyclical contended that the Byzantine church was independent of and equal to the Roman church.

Mosaic depicting Christ as *Pantokrator* (Ruler of All) in the dome of the Church at Daphni, Greece, made in the 11th century

her help, the conspirators, led by John Tzimisces of Armenia, stole into the imperial bedroom while the ascetic basileus was sleeping on a rug on the floor. They kicked him awake and stabbed him to death.

The Rival Bulgarian Empire

In the seventh century, Bulgar tribesmen of Turkic origin invaded Lower Moesia, a Balkan province of the Byzantine Empire.

Michael Rangabe is crowned emperor by the patriarch Nicephorus in this Byzantine painting. During his reign, Crete and Sicily were captured from the Byzantines by the Arabs.

They had formed their own empire by the ninth century. Khan Krum (who reigned 803-814) resoundingly defeated a Byzantine army in 811 and nearly took Constantinople in 813. In 864, Boris I (reigning 852-889) was persuaded by the Byzantine Emperor Michael III to make Christianity Bulgaria's official religion. In 870, when Pope Adrian II would not make Bulgaria an archbishopric, Boris committed Bulgaria to Eastern Orthodoxy.

Boris's son Simeon brought Bulgaria to the zenith of its power through superb administration and successful military campaigns, most notably against the Byzantines and the Magyars. He declared himself czar of the Greeks as well as the Bulgars in 925 and went on to take Serbia the next year. Yet he introduced Byzantine culture to his own empire and sponsored Slavic advances in education, particularly the work of Slavs Saint Cyril and his brother Saint Methodius. The first written Slavic language, Old Church Slavonic, and the Cyrillic alphabet were adopted during his reign. Greatly influenced by its dominant Slavic population, Bulgaria would become the center for Slavic culture in Europe in the tenth and eleventh centuries.

John I Tzimisces of Armenia (924-76)

After Simeon, Bulgaria declined. Its capital Sophia and the royal family were captured in 969 by Russians. The new Byzantine emperor John I Tzimisces intervened in 970, forcing the Russians out of Bulgaria in 972 and annexing the eastern part of Bulgaria to his empire. Samuel, the son of a Bulgarian governor, was made ruler of western Bulgaria four years later.

A notable general under Nicephorus Phocas, he campaigned simultaneously against the Muslims in Mesopotamia and Syria from 972 to 975. In 972, he arranged his supporter Theophano's marriage to the Holy Roman emperor Otto II in an effort to better east-west relations. He ruled until his death in 976.

Basil II (958?-1025)

Basil II, son of Romanus II and stepson of Nicephorus, succeeded, reigning jointly with his brother Constantine VIII. Constantine took no active role. The greatest of the Macedonian emperors, Basil II ruled until 1025, regaining territory in southeastern Asia Minor, Greece, Macedonia, and Thrace and expanding external trade in the Mediterranean and the Black Seas.

Basil succeeded in taking Armenia, threatening Byzantium from the east and destroying the Bulgarian Empire in the west. He waged war on the Bulgars for some twenty years, finally defeating its czar Samuel in 1014. He owed his fame and the nickname of *Bulgaroctonus* (Killer of Bulgars) to the terrifying way he dealt with Samuel's army. He had the eyes of 14,000 Bulgarian soldiers gouged out, with the exception of one soldier in a hundred allowed to keep one eye to lead the others home. In midwinter, Basil threw this blinded army out of the country. When he saw it hobbling home, Samuel had a heart attack.

Basil incorporated the state into his empire in 1018 but he could not stop the increasing takeover of land by the church and a small number of wealthy families.

They came to constitute a separate class of great influence in both government and army. Basil II required every landowner to prove that his land had been lawfully acquired. If he could not, he lost the land. The law reduced many families to poverty but the emperor did not succeed in eliminating the threat of the large landowners. They would play a large part in the eventual fall of the empire.

Zoe's Emperors

After the death of Basil in 1025, the Byzantine Empire continued its economic growth and enjoyed a period of prosperity but remained largely isolated from the rest of the world. Major cultural and scientific advancements were occurring in western Europe and the Muslim east while Constantinople languished under inadequate political leadership. The fifty-year-old princess Zoe occupied a key position, suddenly allowed to say who could wear the imperial purple. She made a choice unfortunate for them both in the domineering Romanus III, prefect of Constantinople. When he reduced Zoe's allowance, the empress had him drowned in his own bath. On the same day, she married her lover Michael, making the notorious pleasure-seeker the emperor. After seven years of bad administration, Michael IV had an epileptic attack. He regarded it as divine punishment and exchanged the imperial robes for a monk's habit. He died soon afterward. Zoe adopted his nephew Michael as her son and heir. When he tried to lock her up in a nunnery, a popular uprising broke out on her behalf. It cost Michael his eyes as well as his throne. Zoe was then permitted to choose yet again. This time she selected a high official named Constantine. His salient characteristic was his inability to take action under any circumstances. The dynasty ended with him.

All emperors after Basil came from the bureaucratic civil service rather than the military. The emperors, not interested in expensive wars or in armies that might threaten their own positions, kept the generals far from the court. The landowners selected as tax collectors sabotaged both, running the imperial coffers and the military out of money by keeping the tax collections for themselves. The military, lacking any organizing force or incentive, progressively deteriorated.

Mid-Byzantine Art: The Macedonian Renaissance

After the ban against icons was lifted in 843, Byzantine art flourished. Coinciding with the new Macedonian dynasty, the period is called the Macedonian Renaissance. Religious icons (the term includes religious art, usually flat, done in oil paint, mosaic, gold, and ivory) were again viewed as an expression of Christian faith. Byzantine artists returned to classical Hellenistic style as the prototype for their paintings. Because it was still not really acceptable to reveal the human body in religious work, they adopted the Greek model of clothing it in clinging drapery that hinted at the figure it covered. This is termed the damp-fold style. They used abstraction, flat patterns or networks of lines, to indicate three dimensional bodies

Emperor Romanus II
(959-963)
and his first wife Eudoxia
being blessed by Christ.
Tenth-century ivory

1265

rather than shading techniques that would have given a greater sense of actual volume. The artistic conventions they developed in an effort to stay within and glorify church convictions remained characteristic of Byzantine art for centuries.

The same was true of their use of mosa-

Miniature from an eleventh-century Byzantine psalter, which depicts Emperor Basil II Bulgaroctonus (Killer of the Bulgars). The emperor is crowned by angels and Christ and worshiped by his subjects, on their knees before him.

ic decoration, which followed a typical pattern linked to that of architecture. The emperor Justinian had encouraged new forms of building. In this mid-Byzantine era, the emphasis was on consolidation. Although inspired by the great dome over a square of the famous Hagia Sophia Church, Middle Byzantine churches tended to be more intimate in scale. There were other important differences. The earlier building used huge curved arches (the pendentives) along the sides of the square to form the transition from it to the domed

roof. The mid-Byzantine churches used much smaller arches at the corners of the square (called squinches) to hold the dome. They also added four equal areas to the sides of the square to form the arms of a cross. This cross-in-the-square church became a common pattern, especially in the eleventh century.

The interior of most such churches was covered with mosaic or painted images of people and events considered sacred. Position indicated the importance of the subjects portrayed. Christ, in full beard, commanded the center of the dome, looking down on all creation. On the rim of the dome and high on the walls were biblical scenes and pictorial anecdotes from the life of Mary. Important saints were depicted on major structural supports, less important ones low down on the walls. In the semidome of the apse, a projection usually on the east side of the church, the Virgin Mary was typically shown carrying the infant Christ. She was venerated in her own right as the Mother of God despite the fact that Byzantine orthodox theology did not subscribe to the doctrine of the immaculate conception.

Orthodoxy considered Pentecost (from the Greek word *pentecoste* for fiftieth) of particular importance. According to the biblical verse 1 John 16:13, it was on the fiftieth day (seventh Sunday) after Easter that the Holy Spirit was given to guide the whole church. Byzantine art depicted it as rays of light from the heavens to the heads of the apostles.

The Battle of Manzikert: 1071
About 1070, new enemies loomed on the eastern borders of the Byzantine Empire. The Abbasidian caliph had long ago been forced to hand over power to Turkish mercenaries. Called Seljuks after their original leader, they established a new nation. Almost immediately after its founding, they began raids into Byzantine territory and Asia Minor. Basileus Romanus IV set after them with his troops, hoping that their large numbers would make up for the lack of quality. He might have succeeded had he been able to count on the loyalty of his officers. In 1071, imperial forces met Turkish at Manzikert. In the course of the battle, treasonous Byzantine officers ordered their rear lines to retreat. This left the front, where Romanus was fighting, unsupported and gave the Turks a free hand. The basileus was captured alive. The defeat was the largest in Byzantium's history and opened up its eastern border.

Godfrey of Bouillon and his crusaders attacking the walls of Jerusalem in the battle that made him the first western ruler in the region.

The Crusades

Wars in the Name of God

"*Deus le vult* (God wills it),'' shouted the crowd on Tuesday, November 27, 1095, from the field outside Clermont. Pope Urban II had summoned the faithful to a council at this French city to present a plan to end Muslim control over Jerusalem and the parts of the Middle East Christians called the Holy Land. He called it a crusade, taking the name from the Latin *crux* (cross) used as its symbol. Four years later,

the defenders of Jerusalem surrendered, but later crusades would continue for more than two hundred years.

Expansion
Originally military in design, the crusades were a response to other factors, as well. They coincided with a return to sovereign control over anarchy and a revived economy evident in larger harvests, increased

The ruins of the crusader's castle in Byblos, Lebanon. This ancient city was captured by the crusaders in 1103.

prosperity and commercial activity, the emergence of European cities, and tremendous population growth. They provided an outlet for trade, an expansion of commercial opportunity, a means of land acquisition, and a place to accommodate the burgeoning population. Generally proclaimed by a pope, they also served the ambition of a series of popes perhaps as eager to expand their own power as to conquer lands and people for the Lord.

Pope Urban II (circa 1040-1099)

Pope Urban II himself encouraged the view that joining up would improve chances of personal salvation. His own enthusiasm and reputation for continuing the reforms of Pope Gregory VII helped advance his cause. Born Odo of Lagery in France, he became prior of the reform-minded Benedictine monastery of Cluny in 1073. He was elected to succeed Gregory VII as the first Cluniac pope in 1088. He served until his death in 1099 and was beatified in 1881. His particular concerns were ending the schism with the Byzantine Christians and reclaiming the Holy Land.

He was delighted when the Byzantine emperor, Alexius I Comnenus, appealed to him in 1095 for help in recovering Anatolia from the Seljuks. The pope blended his concerns in the strategy he outlined at Clermont. Eastern and Western Christianity would fight side by side against the enemy of their faith.

Basileus Alexius I Comnenus (1048-1118)

Alexius I Comnenus had gained the imperial throne in 1081 at a time when the Byzantine Empire was on the brink of ruin, begun with its defeat at the battle at Manzikert a decade earlier. The basileus had promptly joined forces with the Venetians to resist Normans, led by Robert Guiscard, invading Greece. Guiscard had captured Bari, the Italian port city on the Adriatic, in 1071.

By 1090, Seljuk Turks had conquered Syria and Palestine and reclaimed nearly all of Asia Minor from the Byzantines. Nicaea, barely thirty miles (fifty kilometers) from the capital city, was in their hands. In the former strongholds of the imperial army, they formed a Muslim military class that lived off what the conquered Greek, Syrian, and Armenian Christians produced. In Italy and Sicily, Norman Latins had taken over Byzantine possessions.

In 1091, Alexius defeated the Pecheneg Turks encroaching from the north and defused the Seljuk Turks in the East by treaty with them but he knew his only powerful allies were to be found in the West. He worked on improving relations with the Latin Christians, dropping the schism and the tough stance taken since the time of Patriarch Michael Cerularius from the political agenda. (Cerularius went on to proclaim the supremacy of the church over the empire and was dethroned and exiled by Emperor Isaac I Comnenus.)

Interchurch contact was renewed and a solid basis for trust was laid. There was evidence of goodwill on both sides. The pope even lifted the anathema pronounced on the basileus in 1054. The recovery of both churches under the guidance of the pope would enormously improve his image.

Alexius would rule until 1118. In the final decade of the eleventh century, he had his empire under such firm control that he could consider reconquering Anatolia, but only with assistance. Hence, his request to the pope for a contingent of Christian warriors. He guaranteed payment and booty.

The Council of Clermont: 1095
The first one to come forward at the Council of Clermont was Bishop Adhemar of Le Puy. Pope Urban II made him the commander in chief of the First Crusade. *Deus le vult* became its battle cry. The pope outlined his plan. The bishops were to return home and recruit crusaders. Groups of them, each with its own leader and separate financing, would converge in Constantinople and join forces with the Byzantines. Together they would retake Anatolia from its Seljuk conquerors and then proceed to Syria and Palestine.

Popular Armies
The enlistment effort began at once. It largely followed the pope's plan, but he had not anticipated the enthusiasm it would arouse among the common people of Europe. Peasants and city folk, merchants and adventurers alike sewed a cross on their clothing and joined the Peasants' Crusade.

Its largest army was recruited and led by a Picard preacher called Peter the Hermit;

there was another under Gautier Sans-Avoir (Walter the Penniless). With no equipment and few provisions, they set out on a devastating journey east. Their troubles began on the Hungarian border where the king, with little faith in the plunder-hungry bands of crusaders, allowed them passage only under certain conditions, which included no stealing. The undisci-

plined soldiers did not comply, finally making it to Byzantine territory after many skirmishes.

Alexius, recognizing his limited control over these beggarly hordes, had them cross over to Asia Minor in Greek ships. Both armies walked into Turkish ambushes. The surviving crusaders who ended up as slaves in some Oriental market could only count their blessings. Few lived to see the triumph of their cause in Jerusalem.

Pope Urban II presents a charter in this miniature from a twelfth-century manuscript. Prior of Cluny before being elected pope, he inaugurated the First Crusade in 1095.

1269

chūn de son
op de bullon su
ugmie de siegues qi
pour aler coqure la
doultze mer

que la vpicite estoit
presque perdue. Et par
son bel sermon plusieurs
vouerent le saint pelei
nage en la terre doul
tre mer.

Western European
crusaders embarking on
their journey to
Palestine

Pectoral cross
of a knight
participating in the
First Crusade

Anti-Semitism

In the Rhineland, the recruitment effort met with particular success. Great numbers of Christians accepted the pilgrim's cross but the armies they enlisted in fell into the hands of profiteering robber barons. They had discovered quarry closer than the far-away Muslims. To make a good start against the unbelievers, they turned against the Jews, considered suitable victims because they were not baptized, they were often rich, and generally did not take up arms to defend themselves.

This was the first persecution of Jews in German history. The crusaders ransacked the ghettos, the urban areas and villages where they lived, robbing and plundering. It was a peasant crusade on the home front.

Most of the leaders in the region protected the Jews when possible, having commercial ties with them. They knew the movement damaged both their interests.

After plundering the ghettos, the Christians headed east, after Peter and Gauthier. They did not get far. Having learned by experience, the Hungarian king now closed his borders to them and ended their crusade in a bloodbath.

Regular Armies

Five independent armies of noblemen formed by 1096 in response to the pope's call to the crusade. Drawn primarily from France, they also had recruits from Flanders, Lorraine, Burgundy, and southern Italy. Following the pope's concept, they planned to unite at Constantinople. Robert I of Flanders combined groups from Paris and Bruges at Lyons, France, and led them into Italy, crossing the Adriatic at Bari. Raymond of Toulouse took his troops from that city to Lyons, but went on across the top of Italy and down the north shore of the Adriatic. Godfrey of Bouillon went through Hungary, finding less resistance from the Hungarian king than the peasant armies because he could control his troops. The colorful Bohemund of Taranto simply crossed the Adriatic from the Italian port of Brindisi. He was the eldest son of Robert Guiscard, Norman duke of Apulia and Calabria in southern Italy. After Robert Guiscard died in 1085, his domain was divided between Bohemond and his

Crusader with
his horse and standard;
from an English prayer book
from the early thirteenth
century

1271

brother. Bohemond joined the First Crusade to try to extend his possessions. As long as he remained with the crusaders, Bohemond was their leader, although he was not officially recognized as such.

The Bosporus

In November 1096, armies began arriving in Constantinople. The crusaders were not warmly received by the people. They had just gotten rid of the "armies" of Gauthier and Peter. The Greeks and the Franks had long disliked each other and the troops under Count Raymond had plundered a small Greek town on the way. Bohemond had been at war with the Byzantines in Italy, under his father, from 1081 to 1085.

Alexius demanded an oath of allegiance from the leaders. The crusaders were not inclined to give it but the emperor was powerful enough to put pressure on each army in turn. In addition, Alexius required them to turn over any former Byzantine lands they had taken en route. This made them question his overall motive in the crusade. Once the oath was sworn, each new vassal was ferried across the Bosporus with his army, because the next one was about to arrive. This went on through May 1097.

The Conquest of Anatolia

That same month, the crusaders began their first coordinated campaign against Anatolia, besieging the Seljuk Turkish capital at Nicaea. In June, the city surrendered, but only to the Byzantines, not the crusaders. This furthered their suspicion that Alexius planned to use them for his own purposes. Victory came none too soon because the crusaders were already suffering from a serious food shortage. Hunger would continue to be a periodic problem.

On July 1, the crusaders resoundingly defeated the main army of Anatolia at Dorylaeum. The Seljuks offered little further resistance in Asia Minor, unable to stand against the Latin-Byzantine union. After every defeat, they burned the land to prevent their conquerors from living off it, a scorched-earth policy.

Antioch

The crusaders traveled to their next target, the ancient city of Antioch in northern Syria, through a burned and uninhabited area. In the wake of the army, the Byzantines tried to reintroduce their rule.

The Turks had set up an important administrative center at Antioch. It was impossible for the crusaders to pass the city by and head straight for Jerusalem.

A woman bids her crusader husband farewell before he leaves for the Holy Land.

The Second Crusade: 1145-1148

The Christian kingdom of Jerusalem was under constant threat from the Muslims. Divided Islamic forces had begun to unite under the leadership of Imad ad-Din Zangi, the ruler of the territories of Al Mawsil and Halab. In 1144, they reconquered Edessa, putting Jerusalem in a desperate position. In Europe a year later, the pope called for a new crusade to relieve the city. In Germany, his appeal against all opponents of Christianity led to large-scale persecution of the Jews. Holy Roman Emperor Conrad III formed an army to rescue Jerusalem. Bernard of Clairvaux, the monastic refor-

mer under whose leadership the Cistercian order had flourished, stirred up all of France. Louis VII, the king of France, took up the cross and command of an army of his own. In 1147, both armies departed for the Holy Land, as their predecessors had done before. En route, their troops wreaked havoc in the Byzantine Empire.

Only some of the French crusaders made it to Palestine. There they made a strategic error: they decided not to attack the Turks who had conquered Edessa, but the independent city-state of Damascus. The interests of that city and those of the crusaders were, in fact, similar in that Damascus was also being threatened by the Turks. The crusaders' attacks on Damascus in July 1148 were repelled over and over again. The Christians retreated ingloriously all the way to Europe, ending the Second Crusade as the Turks continued their attacks on Jerusalem.

Under Sultan Saladin, who conquered Egypt in 1169, they finally took Jerusalem on October 2, 1187. Pope Gregory VIII responded with a call for a Third Crusade on October 29th. Although it never succeeded in retaking Jerusalem, it did secure a number of cities on the Mediterranean coast, establishing a small Latin kingdom that would last a hundred years.

The leaders of the Second Crusade, Conrad III and Louis VII. Thirteenth-century miniature

Bernard of Clairvaux of France preaches to the Cistercians. Bernard's preaching to secular society prompted many to join the Second Crusade.

They began a siege on October 21, 1097. Antioch fell June 3, 1098. Over the intervening months, the Turks received reinforcements from the East. The fresh troops forced the crusaders back into the city, even occupying the citadel so that the army was threatened from above. Hunger and despair debilitated the crusaders. In Asia Minor, Alexius concluded that all was lost

Mounted crusaders depart for Palestine. Below, the boat they will use to complete the last part of their journey is depicted.

and commanded his troops to withdraw, through a second fury of arson and plundering set by the Turks.

A simple priest arrived on the scene in Antioch and told of a dream in which Saint Andrew showed him the location of the lance used to pierce Christ's side. Whoever possessed the relic would be invincible, he said. The relic was found where he said it would be. Motivated by this miracle, the crusaders fought back, defeating the relief force on June 28. The emir in the citadel surrendered and Christians were delighted to baptize most of his warriors. The rest were allowed free passage.

The crusaders spent the next few months subjecting and ravaging the surrounding countryside and squabbling over the control of Antioch. They had lost the leadership of

Adhemar, the bishop of Le Puy, who had died.

Alexius's claim to Antioch was forgotten. Raymond of Toulouse believed he had right to the city. The quarrel was undoubtedly heightened by the example of Godfrey of Bouillon's brother Baldwin who had taken control of Edessa and created his own principality. The Armenians in the vicinity did not object. The Christian buffer city resulting would resist Turkish assaults for forty years.

The question was resolved in favor of Bohemond, who was given Antioch as a principality. His descendants ruled there until 1268. The Byzantine Empire restricted its expansion after 1098. After being imprisoned by the Muslims for three years (1100-1103), he went to France for help and married the daughter of King Philip I. In 1107, he led an army against the Byzantines in unsuccessful attack. He finally accepted a peace settlement acknowledging Alexius as his overlord in 1108.

Jerusalem

Under the leadership of Godfrey of Bouillon, the remaining crusaders left for their final goal in November 1098. Marching slowly south, they did not now attack fortified positions in order to conserve their forces. The Turks still offered heavy resistance and no more help was expected from Constantinople. The alliance had degenerated. On June 7, 1099, the exhausted army camped at the gates of Jerusalem. After a solemn pilgrimage to the Jordan River, the crusaders attacked.

Jerusalem, under Egyptian control, was ready for a siege, but not of the kind the crusaders mounted, with troop reinforcements from Genoa and new siege machines. On July 15, the Christians invaded Jerusalem and massacred men, women, and children, most of the population. The flowing blood of the Muslims was seen by the crusaders to purify the city. They fought a final battle at Ascalon on August 12, against an Egyptian army, again defeating it. Soon after, most of the crusaders went back to Europe.

The Kingdom of Jerusalem

Godfrey of Bouillon was elected to rule Jerusalem and the conquered territories.

Baldwin of Bouillon, the brother of Godfrey, who took the title first king of Jerusalem after Godfrey's death

1275

Twelfth-century miniature depicting the siege of Antioch. After it was captured, its conqueror Bohemund of Taranto founded a Christian principality there.

each headed for Jerusalem in 1147 with an army. Only some of the French forces made it there. The rest, like most of the German troops, were killed or injured en route. Following an unsuccessful attack launched on Damascus in July 1148, the crusaders gave up and went home.

The Third Crusade: 1187-1192

Zangi had died in 1146, but his policy of Islamic reunification continued under Nur ad-Din, who developed his realm into a major power. Under the legendary Sultan Saladin, its forces conquered Egypt in 1169. After Nur ad-Din's death in 1174, Saladin took over, repeatedly attacking the Christians from three sides for over a decade. In 1187, he entered the kingdom of Jerusalem, taking the Holy City itself on October 2. His holdings now ran from the Tigris River across most of northern Africa. Only the city of Tyre was still Christian.

On October 29, 1187, Pope Gregory VIII called for a Third Crusade. Again, the French king (this time Philip II), the Holy Roman emperor (now Frederick I), and the English king (Richard I) enlisted. They formed the largest army of crusaders since 1095 but could not retake Jerusalem. Frederick never got there, dying in Anatolia. His soldiers retreated to Germany. Philip and Richard were able to secure a number of cities on the Mediterranean, reestablishing a small Latin kingdom that would last a century. No crusade after this would prove as successful. There were many, some designated in history by number and some by name. Some were quite petty.

The Fourth Crusade: 1202-1204

The next crusaders joined the Venetians and a Byzantine usurper to seize Constantinople. In 1204, when the new Byzantine emperor Isaac II Angelus refused to pay them for their services, the crusaders considered themselves justified in plundering the city. Baldwin I of Constantinople succeeded as emperor later that year, after Isaac and his son were killed. He was captured by the Bulgarians at the siege of Adrianople and died in prison in 1205.

Baldwin II inherited the throne at the age of eleven. John of Brienne, former king of Jerusalem, took over as regent until his death in 1237. Baldwin, away in Europe trying to build an army to recover parts of his empire taken by the Greeks and Bulgarians, was only crowned in 1239. He lost Constantinople and the emperorship in

He refused the title of king. He did not want a golden crown "when Christ had worn a thorny crown," he said, and was satisfied with the title "Protector of the Holy Sepulcher." He died only a year later. His brother Baldwin of Edessa was chosen by the nobles of the new realm as successor. Having no objection to a coronation, he became the first king of Jerusalem. Despite its apparent success the kingdom led a difficult existence. It remained an enclave in Turkish territory and was regularly in danger of attack.

The Latin kingdom of Jerusalem was the largest of four states established in the region called the Levant. North of it was Tripoli on the Mediterranean coast, and north of that, Antioch. To the east was Baldwin's Edessa. The existence of those states was doomed.

Most of the success of the First Crusade was due not to the strength of the Christian armies but to the weakness of the Muslims. The Seljuk realm was divided into autonomous states who preferred to fight one another. The situation would reverse once a strong leader presented himself.

The Second Crusade: 1145-1148

Under Imad ad-Din Zangi, the ruler of the territories of Al Mawsil and Halab, the Muslims began to reunite, recapturing Edessa in 1144. The pope announced a Second Crusade a year later. The king of France, Louis VII, and the Holy Roman

1261 to the Byzantine Michael VIII Palaeologus. Baldwin fled to Italy, ending the Latin Empire in the East.

Other Latin states established in Greece as part of the Fourth Crusade would survive some three hundred years. The Palaeologan dynasty Michael VIII founded would continue to reign until 1453, when the Ottoman Turks conquered Byzantine Asia Minor and the Balkans, ending the Byzantine Empire.

The Albigensian Crusade: 1208-1229

The first crusade actually fought in Europe was proclaimed by Pope Innocent III against the Albigenses. Named after their center, the town of Albi in southern France, the Albigenses was the most significant Christian heretical sect of the Middle Ages, based on Cathar beliefs.

It was an outgrowth of the centuries-old Manichaean heresy that posited the separate and competing existence of a god of good and a god of evil. The god of goodness and light they identified with Christ and the New Testament God; the god of evil and darkness, with the Old Testament God and the devil. It was spirit against matter. Spiritual existence or life after death was the goal. The only possible escape from material existence lay in living what they considered a good life. Failure to do so would result in being reborn as a person or an animal. They rejected the normal Christian doctrine of the incarnation.

Cathars lived as either simple believers who had ordinary lives or "perfects," who were ascetics. Considered able to commune with the Lord in prayer, the perfect people were strict vegetarians, not allowed possessions or sexual relations. Simple believers could become perfects through a rite called *consolamentum* (consolation), frequently when they were dying. This involved the refusal of all food and drink.

The heresy had a political aspect to it. Cathars regarded the regular Christian church, with all its corruption, wealth, and interest in material power, as the agent of the devil.

As the property of the Cathars and their sympathizers was confiscated, the Albigensian Crusade resulted in bringing the large territory of southern France under the control of the French crown. The pope laid waste to much of southern France in his brutal crusade to repress the Cathars, but he succeeded.

The Fifth Crusade: 1217-1221

This was not so in the crusade going on in Egypt about the same time. Although the crusaders captured the seaport of Damietta in 1219, they failed to take Cairo and had to give Damietta back in 1221. Expected reinforcements never came and the Christians retreated to Europe.

Holy Roman Emperor Frederick II: 1228-1229

In 1215 and again in 1220, Frederick II vowed to lead a crusade to the Holy Land. He finally left by ship in 1227, but came back to port a few days later, sick. The dis-

The remains of the castle of Sidon in Lebanon. During the first three crusades it was a Muslim fortress, but it fell to the Templars at the beginning of the thirteenth century.

gusted Pope Gregory IX excommunicated him. A year later, Frederick tried again, conducting a crusade through diplomatic negotiation with Egyptian sultan Al-Kamil. He handed over Jerusalem to the emperor and signed a ten-year peace treaty.

Pope Gregory IX, in the meantime, proclaimed his own crusade against the still-excommunicated Frederick and went after his holdings in Italy, forcing Frederick's return there in 1229.

King Louis IX: 1248-1270

The Muslims retook Jerusalem in 1244. French King Louis IX, after planning for four years to take it back, sailed for Cyprus. June 5, 1249, he retook Damietta. His attempt on Cairo the next spring was literally flooded out. The Egyptians opened reservoir sluice gates along the Nile, trapping his army, and forcing Louis's surrender in April 1250. He paid a huge ransom for his own release, gave back Damietta, and crossed the Mediterranean to spend four years consolidating the Latin kingdom in Palestine.

In France in 1270, he tried to mobilize support for a final crusade, against the city of Tunis. Already hampered by lack of interest on the part of the French knights, it ended with his death in Tunisia the same year.

The remaining Christian holdouts in the Middle East fell to the Egyptian Mamluk dynasty. The last was the town of Acre, on May 18, 1291.

Results of the Crusades

The Christians fled to Cyprus and then to Rhodes, where they would remain until the sixteenth century. Once the crusaders were ousted from the Holy Land, there was little response in Europe to further calls to battle. They also left little behind them after all the centuries of bloodshed.

In Europe, the effect was greater. Trade and commercial ties, especially with the cities of Italy, had prospered. The economy as a whole was affected. General awareness of the world and of the potential markets outside Europe had increased. Methods to raise funds for the many crusades fostered the development of new systems of taxation.

In the Byzantine Empire, the crusades permitted the reacquisition of land in Asia Minor but virtually nothing in Syria and Palestine. The East-West Christian alliance led to the granting of preferential trading privileges in the empire to Venice and other Italian cities and the loss of Byzantine control over some of its own trade. The crusaders' sacking of Constantinople in 1204 established the period of Latin rule.

After the First Crusade, castles were erected at strategic locations along the route to the Holy Land to be used as stopover places by the crusaders. This was a way to limit the dangers of the long journey. This castle, Krak des Chevaliers, is located in present-day Syria.

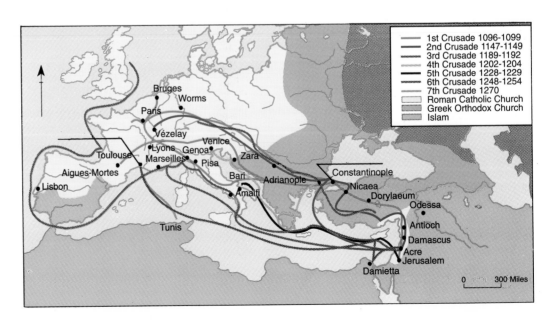

The routes of the seven crusades

1st Crusade 1096-1099
2nd Crusade 1147-1149
3rd Crusade 1189-1192
4th Crusade 1202-1204
5th Crusade 1228-1229
6th Crusade 1248-1254
7th Crusade 1270
Roman Catholic Church
Greek Orthodox Church
Islam

Bruges
Worms
Paris
Vézelay
Venice
Lyons Genoa
Toulouse
Marseilles Pisa
Zara
Aigues-Mortes
Bari
Adrianople
Constantinople
Lisbon
Amalfi
Nicaea
Dorylaeum
Odessa
Tunis
Antioch
Damascus
Acre
Jerusalem
Damietta

0   300 Miles

TIME LINE

WESTERN EUROPE POLITICAL HISTORY	WESTERN EUROPE CULTURAL HISTORY	EVENTS IN THE REST OF THE WORLD

500

510 — **511** Death of Clovis, the first major unifier of the Frankish Empire

520

530

540

550

560

570

580

590

600

610 — **c. 615** The prophet Muhammad founds Islam

620

630

640

650

660

670 — **670** Introduction of the silver *denarius* in the Frankish Empire

680

690 — **687** Majordomo Pépin becomes ruler of core Frankish territories

700 — **c. 700** Christianization of the conquered territories by Anglo-Saxon monks by request of the Frankish rulers — **c. 700** Invention of the art of printing in China

710

720 — **726** Beginning of iconoclasm in the Byzantine Empire

730 — **731** Bede completes *Historia Ecclesiastica gentis Anglorum* (*Religious History of the People of England*)

732 Battle of Poitiers; Charles Martel defeats the Muhammadan army

740

750 — **750** Writing of the *Donatio Constantino* — **c. 750** Muslim conquests reach a climax

751 End of the Merovingian dynasty; Pépin the Short is anointed king — **754** St. Boniface murdered at Dokkum

760

770 — **771** Charlemagne becomes ruler of the entire Frankish Empire — **778** Military defeat of Charlemagne at Zaragoza; later described in the *Chanson de Roland*

780 — **c. 780** Introduction of Carolingian script — **792** Irene becomes empress of the Byzantine Empire

c. 795 Alcuin of York encourages the study of the *artes liberales*

790

800

Prehistory	Antiquity	Middle Ages	Renaissance	Modern History	Contemporary History

WESTERN EUROPE POLITICAL HISTORY	WESTERN EUROPE CULTURAL HISTORY	EVENTS IN THE REST OF THE WORLD

800 The pope crowns Charlemagne emperor in Rome

814 Charlemagne dies; his son Louis the Pious succeeds him

843 The Treaty of Verdun results in the division of the Frankish Empire into three parts

870-880 The treaties of Meerssen and Ribemont divide the central kingdom between the East and West Frankish Empires

c. 900 Weakening of central power

911 Death of the last Carolingian king in the East Frankish Empire; Duke Conrad of the Franks is elected king
919 Henry the Fowler, Duke of Saxony, becomes ruler of the East Frankish Empire

929 Proclamation of the caliphate of Córdoba declared

936 Otto I the Great becomes king of Germany

c. 950 The Ottonian state church system undermines the authority of the secular rulers

955 Otto defeats the Magyars at Lechfeld

962 Otto I is crowned emperor of the Holy Roman Empire

---

c. 800 Introduction of feudalism
802 Centralization of the administrative system following the introduction of the *missi dominici* (imperial envoys)

835 Einhard writes *Vita Karoli Magni*, an autobiography of Charlemagne

855 Paris looted by the Vikings

c. 875 Formalization of the feudal system

c. 900 Ideology of a three-class feudal society

910 Founding of the monastic community at Cluny

c. 930 Odo writes his *Occupation of the Mind*

c. 950 Cultivation of agricultural land, reclamation and deforestation accompanying the growth of the population

---

843 End of iconoclasm

c. 850 Rise of the first Russian kingdom of Novgorod
c. 850 Introduction of paper money in China

c. 900 The Vikings colonize Iceland

Prehistory	Antiquity	Middle Ages	Renaissance	Modern History	Contemporary History

	WESTERN EUROPE POLITICAL HISTORY	WESTERN EUROPE CULTURAL HISTORY	EVENTS IN THE REST OF THE WORLD
970			
980			
990	**987** In the West Frankish Empire, the last Carolingian ruler dies; Hugh Capet becomes king		**990** Russia converts to Christianity, following Byzantine tradition
1000	**c. 1000** The Muslims are driven out of Italy by the Norman armies and withdraw to Sicily	**c. 1000** Córdoba has a population of 50,000	**c. 1000** The Byzantine Empire in its prime
1010	**1002** Otto III dies; Duke Henry of Bavaria ascends the throne		
1020			
1030	**1024** Duke Conrad of Swabia is crowned Holy Roman emperor **c. 1030** The caliphate of Córdoba disintegrates into small principalities		
1040	**1039** Henry III ascends the German throne		
1050	**1045** Henry III sets the bishop of Bamberg on the papal throne as Clement II **c. 1050** Divided Christian states put the Muslims on the Iberian Peninsula on the defensive	**c. 1050** Development of Romanesque architecture	
1060	**1054** The Great Schism divides the Christian church **1059** The popes are chosen by a council of Roman clergymen from this date forward **1071** Norman army led by Robert Guiscard conquers the city of Bari, last Byzantine stronghold in Italy		
1070	**1073** The reformist monk Hildebrand ascends the papal throne as Gregory VII		**1066** Battle of Hastings; William the Conqueror takes England **c. 1075** Seljuks conquer large parts of the Byzantine Empire
1080	**1075** Beginning of the Investiture Controversy, as Gregory VII forbids Henry IV to elect and install bishops **1077** After his excommunication, Henry IV regains his throne in Canosa **1080** The Christians conquer Toledo **1084** After a second anathema, Henry IV elects an antipope and is crowned emperor in Rome	**1075** *Dictatus Papae* (*Dictates of the Pope*) written by Gregory VII **1080** Peace of God movement	
1090	**1085** The reform movement of the Almoravids founds an orthodox empire stretching from Tunis to Toledo **1091** Sicily is captured from the Muslims **1096** The First Crusade departs for Jerusalem	**1094** El Cid conquers Valencia **1095** *Deus le vult* (God wills it) becomes the battle cry of the First Crusade	
1100	**1099** The crusaders capture Jerusalem	**1096** Persecution of Jews in the Holy Roman Empire **1099** Godfrey of Bouillon is crowned king of Jerusalem **c. 1100** Rise of the commercial system of annual fairs	
1110			
1120			
1130	**1122** The Concordat of Worms settles the Investiture Controversy	**1120** The new monastic orders of the Cistercians and Premonstratensians receive papal approval	
1140			

Prehistory	Antiquity	Middle Ages	Renaissance	Modern History	Contemporary History

WESTERN EUROPE POLITICAL HISTORY	WESTERN EUROPE CULTURAL HISTORY	EVENTS IN THE REST OF THE WORLD

1140

1145 The reform movement of the Almohads conquers North Africa

1150

c. 1150 Development of Gothic architecture in the Île de la Cité in Paris

1160

1170

1171 Muslim Spain included in the caliphate of the Almohads

1180

1181 Birth of St. Francis of Assisi

1190

1200

c. 1200 The survival of Christianity on the Iberian Peninsula is secured

1210

c. 1145 Formation of the kingdom of Portugal

1206 Rise of the Mongolian Empire under Genghis Khan

1220

1230

1240

1250

c. 1250 *Reconquista* in full swing

1260

1270

1280

1290

1291 Acre, the last Christian stronghold in the Middle East, falls

1300

1310

Prehistory	Antiquity	Middle Ages	Renaissance	Modern History	Contemporary History

THE BYZANTINE EMPIRE POLITICAL HISTORY	THE BYZANTINE EMPIRE CULTURAL HISTORY	EVENTS IN THE REST OF THE WORLD
	5th and 6th cent. Monophysites disturb the peace in the church	**615** Muhammad founds Islam
c. 650 The Byzantine Empire is threatened by Arab armies and Slavic tribes	**c. 650** Latin is replaced by Greek throughout the Byzantine Empire as the most important language	**c. 650** Invention of the art of printing in China
717 The Arabs are defeated during the siege of Constantinople	**c. 710** The empire flourishes	
730 Imperial edict denouncing icon veneration	**726** Iconoclasm divides the Byzantine Empire	**731** Bede completes the *Historia Ecclesiastica gentis Anglorum* (*Religious History of the English People*)
741 Constantine V becomes emperor	**c. 750** Military fortification and peace in the empire	**c. 750** Zenith of Muslim conquests
780 Irene becomes regent of her underage son		
792 Irene succeeds her son as empress	**790** Temporary restoration of religious images during the seventh council of Nicaea	
802 The empress Irene is deposed by the minister of finance	**c. 810** Stabilization of the economy	**800** Charlemagne is crowned emperor in Rome
820 The Armenian dynasty begins with Michael II	**822** Rebellion of Thomas the Slav; unrest in the empire	
843 End of iconoclasm		
867 The Macedonian dynasty begins with Basil I	**c. 850** Beginning of the Golden Age, characterized by cultural blossoming and political progress	**c. 850** Introduction of paper money in China

Prehistory	Antiquity	Middle Ages	Renaissance	Modern History	Contemporary History

THE BYZANTINE EMPIRE POLITICAL HISTORY	THE BYZANTINE EMPIRE CULTURAL HISTORY	EVENTS IN THE REST OF THE WORLD
	870 Codification of the law by Basil I	**870-80** Frankish Empire breaks up into two parts
	890 *Basilica*, books on imperial law, written by Leo VI	**c. 900** Iceland is colonized by the Vikings
		919 Henry the Fowler ascends the German throne
	c. 920 Struggle against the power of the large landowners	**929** Caliphate of Córdoba
944 Constantine Porphyrogenitus becomes emperor following a palace revolution	**c. 950** Cultural renaissance under Constantine; *Book of Ceremonies* written	**962** Otto I becomes Holy Roman emperor
		c. 990 Russia converts to Christianity
c. 1000 The empire reaches its greatest size under Basil II	**1000** Byzantine Empire at the height of its power	
	c. 1025 Disintegration of the empire	**c. 1030** End of the Caliphate of Córdoba
1054 The Great Schism divides the Christian church	**1050** Papal bull on the altar of the Hagia Sophia Church	**1066** Battle of Hastings; William the Conqueror takes England
1071 Battle of Manzikert; the Byzantine army is defeated by the Seljuks	**c. 1075** Collapse of political power in and outside the empire	**1096** The First Crusade departs for Jerusalem **1099** The crusaders conquer Jerusalem

870 — 880 — 890 — 900 — 910 — 920 — 930 — 940 — 950 — 960 — 970 — 980 — 990 — 1000 — 1010 — 1020 — 1030 — 1040 — 1050 — 1060 — 1070 — 1080 — 1090 — 1100

Prehistory	Antiquity	Middle Ages	Renaissance	Modern History	Contemporary History

Glossary

Adelaide widowed queen of Lombardy who, in 951, asked Otto the Great for aid against the usurper Berengar II, making possible Otto's rise to power.

Aethelred the Unready (c. 968–1016) Anglo-Saxon king of England (978–1016) called "The Unready" from the Old English *unraed* (bad counsel). His marriage to Emma, daughter of Richard II, duke of Normandy, laid the basis for the Norman claim to the English throne.

Alcuin (or Albinus) (735–804) Anglo-Saxon scholar and abbot of St. Martin of Tours; at the request of Charlemagne, initiated the Carolingian Renaissance between 781 and 790.

Alexius I Comnenus (1048–1118) Byzantine emperor (1081–1118). His request to Urban II for troops to fight the Muslims sparked the First Crusade in 1095.

Alfred the Great (849–899) king of the West Saxons (871–899); king of England (886–899). He provided the basis for English unification.

Almohads Islamic reformers from North Africa who drove the Almoravids out of southern Spain between 1146 and 1269, establishing a strong caliphate.

Almoravids a fundamentalist Muslim tribe from the southern Sahara who conquered North Africa and aided the Muslims in Córdoba against the Christians between 1086 and 1146.

Anglo-Saxons Germanic tribes made up of Angles, Saxons, and Jutes living in England before the Norman conquest. They gradually conquered Britain over the fifth century.

Antioch (Antaka) founded in 301 BC by Seleucus I, it was the capital city of Syria until Rome's conquest of Syria in 64 BC. In the eleventh century, it was a Muslim center of government. The Christians conquered it in 1098 during the First Crusade, establishing it as a Christian principality under Bohemund of Taranto.

Aragon a Christian kingdom in northeastern Spain, south of the Pyrenees.

Armenia a region in southwestern Asia south of the Caucasus Mountains.

Armenian emperors a succession of Byzantine emperors between 813 and 842, begun by Leo V.

Austrasia a Frankish kingdom in the seventh century, the eastern part of the original Merovingian Empire.

Baldwin (Boudewijn) with the Iron Arm first count of Flanders (863–879), he defended it against the Vikings. Abducting and marrying the daughter of Charles the Bald, he founded a dynasty of Baldwins in Flanders lasting through the eleventh century.

Baldwin I (of the Latin Empire) (1172–1205) first Latin emperor of Constantinople (1204–1205), born in France.

Baldwin I (of Jerusalem; Boudewijn of Bouillon) (1058–1118) king of Jerusalem (1100–1118), brother of Godfrey of Bouillon and a leader in the First Crusade. In 1098, he conquered Edessa and set up a Christian stronghold there.

Baldwin II (of the Latin Empire) (1217–1273) last Latin emperor of Constantinople (1228–1261).

Baldwin II (of Jerusalem) (?–1131) king of Jerusalem (1118–1131), cousin and successor of Baldwin of Bouillon.

Baldwin III (c. 1130–1162) Latin king of Jerusalem (1143–1162). He lost Damascus in 1154 to Nur ad-Din, Turkish ruler of Aleppo.

Basil II (c. 958–1025) Byzantine emperor (963–1025), called *Bulgaroctonus* (Killer of Bulgars), most powerful of the Macedonian dynasty.

basileus (king) title of the Byzantine emperor, regarded as the head of Christendom and God's representative on Earth.

Battle of Manzikert 1071 defeat marking the end of Byzantine imperial power in Asia Minor.

Bernard of Clairvaux, St. (1090–1154) a Cistercian monk who summoned the French for the Second Crusade in 1146. Canonized in 1174.

Bohemund of Taranto (1052–1111) son of the Norman duke Robert Gestured and a leader in the First Crusade. In 1098, established a kingdom in conquered Antioch.

Bulgaria constituted the strongest empire in eastern Europe in the ninth and early tenth centuries. Incorporated into the Byzantine Empire in 1018, Bulgaria rebelled in 1185, forming another empire which collapsed over the fourteenth century.

Byzantium (Constantinople) rebuilt and renamed by Constantine the Great in 313. Also called the New Rome (*Nova Roma*), it was capital of the Byzantine Empire and residence of the emperor until its fall in 1453.

caliph title taken by Muhammad's successors as secular rulers and religious leaders of Muslim states.

Caliphate of Córdoba Islamic state in Spain (929–1031) first proclaimed by Emir Abd al-Rahmon III.

Capet, Hugh (c. 938–996) king of France (987–996). Founder of the Capetian dynasty that united France and lasted until 1328.

Caroline minuscule a script introduced during the Carolingian Renaissance to replace the illegible Merovingian handwriting. It formed the basis for lowercase letters of the Latin alphabet.

Carolingian Renaissance a Frankish revival of Roman culture in the late eighth and ninth centuries, reorganizing education and reviving art and literature.

Carolingians Frankish dynasty of kings and emperors, called Carolingian after *Carolus,* the Latin form of Charlemagne.

Castile originally a Christian kingdom in northern Spain, in the eleventh century it annexed León and spread Castilian culture throughout Spain.

castle fortified farmstead built by a feudal lord to protect himself and his serfs against raids. Originally wooden towers, by the thirteenth century, castles were commonly huge stone strongholds.

cavalry mounted soldiers.

Charlemagne (Charles the Great) (742–814) Frankish king (768–814) and Holy Roman emperor (800–814). He established the Holy Roman Empire.

Charles II (the Bald) (823–877) Holy Roman emperor (875–877), king of France (as Charles I, 843–877), fourth son of Holy Roman emperor Louis I.

Charles Martel (The Hammer) (c. 688–741) ruler of the Frankish kingdom of Austrasia (719–741), illegitimate son of Pépin of Herstal and grandfather of Charlemagne.

Cluny abbey in Burgundy founded by William of Aquitaine in 910 and put under direct papal authority to prevent influence by nobles and corrupt bishops; noted for church reform. Many monasteries were founded under its auspices.

Concordat of Worms 1122 compromise between Pope Calixtus II and Holy Roman emperor Henry V on investiture. The church was accorded the right to elect and invest bishops but only in the presence of the emperor who retained the right to confer any land and wealth attached to the bishopric.

Conrad II of Swabia (c. 990–1039) king of Germany (1024–1039); Holy Roman emperor (1027–1039); king of the Lombards (1026). In 1033, he inherited the kingdom of Burgundy.

Constantine VI Byzantine emperor (780–797), son of Emperor Leo IV and Irene, who seized power and blinded him.

Constantine VII Porphyrogenitus (905–959) Byzantine emperor (908–959).

Córdoba (Spain) important in Phoenician and Carthaginian times, and a Roman settlement from the first century BC to its capture by the Visigoths in 572. Taken by the Muslims in 711, made capital of Muslim Spain in 756.

corvée the work carried out by serfs on feudal estates.

Council of Clermont the public meeting called by Pope Urban II in 1095 to announce the First Crusade.

count loyal vassal who received land in fief from a Carolingian ruler.

crusades military expeditions undertaken by Christians from the end of the eleventh to the end of the thirteenth century, primarily to recover the Holy Land from Muslim control.

Damascus ancient capital of a city-state in Roman times; conquered variously by David of Israel, Assyrian Tiglath-pileser III in 732 BC, and Alexander the Great in 333–332 BC; part of the Seleucid Kingdom until taken by Pompey the Great in 64 BC. Made a Christian bishopric in the first century AD, it was taken over by Muslims in 635 and Turks in 1056. Damascus was besieged but not taken by the Christians (in 1148). In 1154, it fell to the Egyptians. It was the headquarters of Saladin, sultan of Egypt and Syria, during the Third Crusade.

danegeld a direct tax introduced by Aethelred the Unready, Anglo-Saxon king of England, paid as annual tribute to the Vikings (Danes).

Danelaw a Viking kingdom in northeast England.

Donatio constantini (Donation of Constantine) eighth-century forged last will and testament of Constantine the Great, leaving the western part of his kingdom to the pope; basis for papal demand for authority over the rulers of Europe.

Eastern Frankish Empire acquired by Louis the German in 843, consisting of the tribal dukedoms of Bavaria, Saxony, Swabia, the Franks, and Lotharingia.

Edessa a city in Syria conquered by Baldwin of Bouillon in 1098; established as a Christian principality; recaptured in 1145, leading to the Second Crusade.

Einhard (c. 770–840) Frankish scholar and monk, biographer of Charlemagne.

El Cid (c. 1040–1099) *El Cid Campeador* (The Lord Champion), born Rodrigo Díaz de Vivar; Spanish legendary warrior.

emissary counts trusted men sent by Carolingian rulers to monitor the policy of regional counts and to hear the appeals of the people in the region.

feudalism the economic, political, and social system of medieval Europe in which power was based on land ownership and loyalty. Vassals held large landed estates, worked by serfs, in return for allegiance, military, and other services they paid the landowners or overlords.

First Crusade (1096–1099) under Godfrey of Bouillon and Raymond of Toulouse, crusaders conquered Edessa, Tripoli, Antioch, and Jerusalem, making them Christian kingdoms.

Flanders a region on the North Sea coast made part of his empire by Charlemagne in the ninth century. Under independent counts, it developed into a regional power. In the eleventh century, the courts of Flanders were vassals for both the French crown and the Holy Roman Empire.

Franks Germanic tribesmen who established the Frankish Empire.

free area a settlement inhabited by tradesmen and craftsmen that did not fall within the feudal structure and had its own administrative and legal system.

Frisians Germanic tribesmen who settled on the Waddenzee and the North Sea coast in the sixth century. Defeated by Charles Martel; completely subjected by 785.

gau land given in fief to a loyal vassal, held by him in return for allegiance and services rendered to the landowner.

Godfrey of Bouillon (1060–1100) duke of Lower Lotharingia and leader of the First Crusade. He took part in the capture of Jerusalem in 1099, ruling it as Protector of the Holy Sepulchre, refusing to be crowned king.

Granada a small mountain state in southern Spain where the last of the Muslims held out against the Christians until 1492.

Greek the language of Greece, used by the Byzantine Empire from the seventh century on.

Gregory VI pope (1045–1046). He bought the papal office from Benedict IX and subsequently used his wealth to repel corruption.

Gregory VII, St. (Hildebrand) (c. 1020–1085) pope (1073–1085), canonized in 1606. His effort to reform the medieval church is called Gregorian Reform. He insisted on the primacy of church over state, challenging lay investiture.

hajib title of the highest ranking civil servant under the caliph in Córdoba; also used by rulers of the small states.

Henry II of Bavaria (973–1024) called Henry the Saint because of his piety; king of Germany (1002–1024), king of the Lombards (1004–1024), and Holy Roman emperor (1014–1024). Elected by German

nobles to succeed Otto III, he was supporter of Cluniac reform. He was canonized in 1146.

Henry III (The Black) (1017–1056) king of Germany (1028–1056) and Holy Roman emperor (1039–1056). Son and successor of Conrad II, he was an advocate of Cluniac reform but retained his authority over the church.

Henry IV (1050–1106) king of Germany (1056–1106) and Holy Roman emperor (1084–1106). He succeeded his father Emperor Henry III at age six; his mother ruled as regent. He was excommunicated by Pope Gregory VII in 1076 over the issue of lay investiture. In 1077, he did penance outside the castle at Canossa, was reinstated, and was excommunicated again in 1080. He deposed the pope in 1081.

Henry the Fowler of Saxony (c. 876–936) king of Germany (919–936). He united the German Empire.

Holy Roman Empire title adopted in the thirteenth century in an effort to reinstitute the Roman Empire. Mainly comprised of German states, its first emperor, Otto the Great, was crowned in 962. By 1100, the empire included the kingdoms of Italy, Bohemia, Burgundy, and Germany. It lasted until 1806.

iconoclasm from the Greek *eikon* (image) and *kloein* (break); a movement originating in the Byzantine Empire in the eighth and ninth centuries that condemned the veneration of various forms of artwork called icons.

iconodouloi (icon defenders, or servants of images) supporters, including the Roman papacy, of the view that regarded icons as an acceptable form of Christian worship.

immunity feudal independence from the authority of local civil servants.

investiture a ceremony in which the symbols of office are conferred on a prelate (church official).

investiture controversy a major dispute in the eleventh and twelfth centuries over lay investiture, the role played by secular nobility in the ceremonies putting church officials (prelates) in office. It was resolved in favor of the church at the Concordat of Worms in 1122.

Irene (752–803) empress of the Byzantine Empire (797–802). Married to Emperor Leo IV in 769, and regent for her son Constantine VI (780–790 and 792–797), whom she imprisoned and blinded. Deposed by Nicephorus and exiled to the island of Lésvos. She summoned the Council of Nicaea in 787 to restore image worship.

Isaurian dynasty founded by Leo III the Isaurian, it ruled the Byzantine Empire (717–802).

Jerusalem ancient city in Palestine sacred to Jews, Christians, and Muslims.

John Orphanotropus eunuch who governed the Byzantine Empire from 1034 to 1042 through Emperor Michael IV and his cousin Michael V, adopted by Zoe. Their reign, characterized by extortion, was ended by popular revolt.

John XII (c. 937–964) pope (955–964). Called the boy pope because he was elected at eighteen, he crowned Otto the Great emperor in 962. He refused allegiance to Otto in 963 and was deposed.

kadi a government official in the caliphate of Córdoba charged with caring for the poor and public works in provincial capitals.

Latin official and literary language in Western Europe. As a result of poverty and war, its use declined as education deteriorated. During the Carolingian Renaissance, both revived.

Leo III the Isaurian (c. 680–741) Byzantine emperor (717–741), restored government after near anarchy, deposing Emperor Theodosius III. Noted for his defense of Constantinople and his ban on icon veneration which led to his excommunication in 731.

Leo III, St. (c. 750–816) pope (795–816). In 800, he crowned Charlemagne emperor of the West, ending eastern influence on the western papacy. He retained religious control despite imperial intervention.

Leo IX (1002–1054) pope (1049–1054). His exchange with Michael I Cerularius (patriarch of Constantinople) of anathemas and mutual excommunication in 1054 (called the Great Schism) was the culmination of long theological dispute between eastern and western Christians.

Leo V the Armenian Byzantine emperor from 813 to 820.

León tenth-century Christian kingdom in northwestern Spain; absorbed by Castile in the eleventh century.

Lombards a Germanic people who invaded and settled in northern Italy in the sixth century.

Lothar I (c. 795–855) Holy Roman emperor (840–855), eldest son of Holy Roman Emperor Louis I, the Pious, and grandson of Charlemagne. Made coruler with his father in 817, he twice revolted against him with his brothers, Louis the German and Charles the Bald. He then battled them and lost at the Battle of Fontenay in 841. Lothar received Italy in 822, the eastern part of the empire in 839, and guarantee to the title of Holy Roman emperor and sovereignty over Italy, Burgundy, Alsace, Lorraine, and the Low Countries by the Treaty of Verdun in 843.

Louis II (c. 825–875) Holy Roman emperor (855–875) and king of Italy (844–875).

First son of Holy Roman emperor Lothar I.

Louis II the German (c. 806–876) king of Germany (840–876), the third son of Holy Roman emperor Louis I. The Treaty of Verdun gave him absolute power over the Eastern Frankish Empire in 843. He went on to take eastern Lorraine in 870.

Louis I the Pious (778–840) Holy Roman emperor (814–840), king of France (814–840), king of Germany (814–840), and king of Aquitaine (781–840). Son and sole successor of Charlemagne, as central authority in the kingdom disintegrated his sons Lothar I, Louis II (Louis the German), Pépin of Aquitaine, and Charles II (Charles the Bald, his son by a second marriage) struggled for power.

Macedonians dynasty of Byzantine emperors (842–1025) named after Basil I the Macedonian.

Magyars Hungarians; originally an Asiatic mounted people, they settled in the Danube region at the end of the ninth century and invaded the Eastern Frankish Empire; conquered in 955 by Otto the Great.

majordomo (mayor of the palace) originally, the hereditary office of royal steward in the Frankish Empire. As Merovingian power weakened, they were used as royal ministers until 751.

marks (or marches) military districts on the borders of the Carolingian Empire to provide protection against invasion; governed by counts, with the title margrave or marquise. The Danish March became Denmark.

Mercia Anglo-Saxon kingdom that once occupied most of southern England.

Merovingians rulers of the Frankish Empire from the fifth century, named after Meroveus, the grandfather of Clovis I.

Michael II Byzantine emperor (820–829); an officer of the Armenikoi elite corps; planned the murder of Leo V.

Middle Byzantine Empire former Eastern Roman Empire, from 843 (the reestablishment of the veneration icons) to 1204 (when the Crusaders occupied Constantinople).

mustasib government official in the caliphate of Córdoba responsible for trade.

Navarre Christian kingdom in northern Spain. Pushed into the Pyrenees over the eleventh century, it became increasingly involved in French politics. Its last king, Henry IV, was the founder of the French royal dynasty of the Bourbons.

Neustria Frankish kingdom in the seventh century, consisting of the western region of the original Merovingian Empire; reunited with Austrasia in 687.

Nicephorus I Byzantine emperor (802–811). He deposed Irene and restored iconoclasm.

Nicephorus II Phocas Byzantine emperor (963–969).

Nithard Frankish scholar and monk at the time of the Carolingian Renaissance.

Normandy area in western Gaul given in fief to the Normans in 911 where they established a mighty empire. The Norman duke William the Conqueror conquered England in 1066. Norman nobles established a kingdom in southern Italy and on Sicily in 1029.

Normans "North men," or Vikings, Nordic people (Danes, Swedes, and Norwegians) who variously raided, traded, and settled on the coasts and rivers of Europe, Greenland, and North America in the eighth and ninth centuries.

Oaths of Strasbourg oaths of alliance sworn in 842 by Charles the Bald and Louis the German against Lothar I.

Odo, St. (c. 879–944) second abbot of Cluny, he turned the monastery into a model community, abolishing simony and corruption. He sought to have the church share power in the empire with the secular rulers.

Offa king of Mercia (757–796). He controlled the Anglo-Saxon kingdoms in southern England, fostering English unification.

Otto I the Great (912–973) Holy Roman emperor (962–973), king of Germany (936–973). The son of German king Henry I, he became ruler of Italy by marrying Adelaide, the widowed queen of Lombardy. He deposed Pope John XII and had Leo VIII elected in 963.

Outremer name given to the Christian kingdoms in Palestine after the First Crusade.

patriarch title accorded the heads (bishops) of the five main sections (called *sees*) of the Christian church: Rome (in the West) and Alexandria, Antioch, Constantinople, and Jerusalem (in the East). Those in the East viewed the pope as the patriarch of Rome, gave him primacy of honor, but did not accept Rome's claims for supremacy in church matters.

Peace of God informal code of honor between the church and medieval sovereigns to protect the people against plundering and murder.

Peasants' Crusade popular response to the First Crusade in 1096. Urged on by Peter the Hermit and led by Walter the Penniless.

Pépin of Herstal (c. 635–c. 714) majordomo (mayor of the palace) of Austrasia. In 687, he defeated his Neustrasian counterpart and gained power over the united Frankish Empire.

Pépin the Short (c. 714–768) mayor of the palace of Austrasia (741–751) and king of the Franks (751–768), son of Charles Martel, and grandson of Pépin of Herstal. In 751, Pépin deposed Childeric, becoming the 1287 first Carolingian king. Crowned by Pope Stephen II (III) in 754, he defeated the Lombards in northern Italy and gave the pope their territories, including Ravenna. Called the Donation of Pépin, it was the basis for the Papal States.

Portugal the region given to Henry of Burgundy and his wife, Theresa, in 1093 by King Alfonso I of Castile. Their son Alfonso Henriques rebelled against Theresa in 1128 and was granted the throne as Alfonso I by the dominant Portuguese nobility in 1143. The kingdom gained papal recognition in 1179.

Raymond of Toulouse (1042–1105) a southern French nobleman and one of the leaders in the First Crusade.

Reconquista the recapture of Muslim-occupied Spain by Christians beginning in the eleventh century.

Robert Guiscard (1015–1085) Norman conqueror of Calabria and Apulia in southern Italy. A vassal of the pope, he was appointed duke. His brother Roger I conquered Sicily.

Roger I (c. 1031–1101) Norman conqueror of Sicily, he took from 1061 to 1091 to win the region from the Byzantines.

Roger II (1095–1154) first king of Sicily (1130–1154). Second son of Roger I, he pieced together a kingdom from inherited titles as count of Sicily (1103) and duke of Apulia (by 1129). Claiming sovereignty in 1130 over the southern Italian regions of Calabria, Capua, and Naples, he established a realm that would last seven centuries. He encouraged religious diversity and peace.

Romanus IV Diogenes Byzantine emperor (1068–1071), betrayed by his own officers at the Battle of Manzikert in 1071, he was defeated and taken prisoner by the Seljuks.

Saracens Like *Moors*, a pejorative term for Arab Muslims, in medieval texts. They set up the caliphate of Córdoba and were seen by the Christians as a continuous threat.

Second Crusade (1147–1149) authorized by the pope and preached by Bernard of Clairvaux in 1146, after the Turks had conquered Edessa and threatened Jerusalem. The Christians unsuccessfully besieged Damascus and returned home empty-handed.

Seljuks Turkish clan converted to Islam in the tenth century; major dynasty in the Middle East over the eleventh and twelfth centuries. Under Sultan Togrul Beg, protector of the Sunni Muslim caliph of Baghdad, they established an empire in Persia between 1040 and 1055. Opposed by Shia Muslims and Christian Byzantines, Seljuks Alp Arslan and Malik Shah entered Syria, Palestine, and Anatolia. This and Alp Arslan's victory at the Battle of Manzikert (1071) was rationale for the First Crusade.

serfs peasant farmers dependent on their feudal lords, they performed unpaid labor (*corvée*) and exchanged their personal freedom and part of their harvest for a small plot of land and protection.

Sicily Mediterranean island where Muslims established a center of Islamic culture in the ninth century; ousted by the Normans in 1061.

simony the sale of clerical office for money.

Song of Roland an epic poem among the first literary works in many European languages about the death of Roland, one of Charlemagne's commanders.

Thomas the Slav (?–823) a Slavic officer who led an army of discontented farmers and adventurers against Byzantine emperor Michael II. He laid siege to Byzantium, with Muslim support. He was captured and killed while fleeing a Bulgarian attack.

treasury term used for royal lands used to finance a Carolingian king's policy.

Treaty of Meerssen (870) divided the northern part of Lothar I's empire between Charles the Bald and Louis the German.

Treaty of Verdun (843) following the Battle of Fontenay in 841, it divided up the Carolingian Empire. Charles the Bald received the West, Louis the German the East, and Lothar I guarantee to the title of Holy Roman emperor and sovereignty over Italy, Burgundy, Alsace, Lorraine, and the Low Countries.

tribal dukedoms the territories of Bavaria, Saxony, Swabia, and the Franks in eastern Francia where ancient tribal traditions inhibited feudalism.

Umayyads clan of Arab tribes based in Mecca who founded the first Muslim dynasty (661–750) of Córdoba. They established an Islamic kingdom in Spain in 756. In 929, they set up the caliphate of Córdoba and ruled until 1031.

Urban II (1040–1099) pope (1088–1099) His 1095 proclamation at Clermont initiated the First Crusade.

vassals men who swore allegiance to a patron landowner and owed him services in exchange for protection and land.

Bibliography

The Frankish Empire

Bachrach, B. S. *Merovingian Military Organization 481–751*. Minneapolis, 1972.

Geary, P. J. *Before France and Germany: The Creation and Transformation of the Merovingian World*. Cambridge, 1988.

James, E. *The Franks*. Oxford, 1988.

Leyser, K. J. *The Ascent of Latin Europe*. Oxford, 1986.

Reuter, T., ed. *The Medieval Nobility:Studies on the Ruling Classes of France and Germany from the Sixth to the Twelfth Century*. Amsterdam/New York/Oxford, 1979.

Wallace–Hadrill, J. M. *The Barbarian West*. New York, 1962.

———. *The Long–haired Kings and Other Studies in Frankish History*. London, 1962.

Wood, I., and P. Sawyer. *Early Medieval Kingship*. Leeds, 1977.

Wood, I. *The Merovingian Kingdoms, 450–751*. London/New York, 1993.

Charlemagne

Collins, R. *Early Medieval Spain*. London, 1983.

Ganshof, F. L. *The Carolingians and the Frankish Monarchy*. London, 1971.

Halphen, F. L. *Charlemagne and the Carolingian Empire*. Amsterdam/New York/London, 1977.

Hodges, R., and D. Whitehouse. *Mohammed, Charlemagne and the Origins of Europe*. London, 1983.

McKitterick, R. *The Frankish Kingdoms under the Carolingians*. London/New York, 1983.

———, ed. *Carolingian Culture: Emulation and Innovation*. Cambridge, 1994.

Nelson, J. L. *Politics and Ritual in Early Medieval Europe*. London, 1986.

Pirenne, H. *Mohammed and Charlemagne*. London, 1939.

Reuter, T. *Germany in the Early Middle Ages, 800–1056*. London/New York, 1991.

The Western Empire

Bullough, D. *The Age of Charlemagne*. London, 1965.

Cabaniss, A. *Son of Charlemagne: A Contemporary Life of Louis the Pious*. Syracuse, 1961.

Duckett, E. S. *Alcuin, Friend of Charlemagne*. New York, 1951.

Godman, P. *Poetry of the Carolingian Renaissance*. London, 1985.

Godman, P., and R. Collins, eds. *Charlemagne's Heir: New Perspectives on the Reign of Louis the Pious*. Oxford, 1986.

Hodges, R. *The Anglo-Saxon Achievement*. London, 1989.

Laistner, M. L. W. *Thought and Letters in Western Europe, AD 500–900*. London, 1931.

Nelson, J. L. *Charles the Bald*. London/New York, 1992.

McKitterick, R. *The Carolingians and the Written Word*. Cambridge, 1989.

Sawyer, P. *The Age of the Vikings*. London, 1962.

Ullmann, W. *The Carolingian Renaissance and the Idea of Kingship*. London, 1969.

Wallach, L. *Alcuin and Charlemagne*. Ithaca, 1959.

Feudalism

Beeler, J. *Warfare in Feudal Society*. Ithaca, 1971.

Brønsted, J. *The Vikings*. Harmondsworth, 1960.

Cheyette, F. L. *Lordship and Community in Medieval Europe*. New York, 1968.

Duby, G. *The Three Orders: Feudal Society Imagined*. Chicago, 1980.

Herlihy, D. *The History of Feudalism*. New York, 1971.

Odegaard, C. *Vassi and Fideles in the Carolingian Empire*. Cambridge, 1945.

Sawyer, P. *Kings and Vikings: Scandinavia and Europe, AD 700–1100*. London, 1982.

Southern, R. W. *The Making of the Middle Ages*. London, 1953.

The Feudal Society

Boch, M. *Feudal Society*. London, 1961.

Ganshof, F. L. *Feudalism*. London, 1952.

Hamilton, B. *Religion in the Medieval West*. London, 1986.

Knowles, D. *Christian Monasticism*. London, 1969.

Lawrence, C. H. *Medieval Monasticism*. London/New York, 1989.

Rosenwein, B. *Rhinocerous Bound: Cluny in the Tenth Century*. Philadelphia, 1982.

Southern, R. W. *Western Society and the Church in the Middle Ages*. Harmondsworth, 1970.

Strayer, J. R. *Feudalism*. New York, 1965.

Ullmann, W. *The Growth of Papal Government in the Middle Ages*. London, 1955.

Early Medieval Politics

Blumenthal, U. *The Investiture Contest*. Philadelphia, 1988.

Hallam, E. H. *Capetingian France, 987–1328*. New York, 1980.

Kantorowicz, E. *The King's Two Bodies*. Princeton, 1957.

Leyser, K. J. *Rule and Conflict in an Early Medieval Society: Ottonian Saxony*. Bloomington, 1979.

Painter, S. *The Rise of the Feudal Monarchies*. Ithaca, 1951.

Robinson, I. S. *Authority and Resistance in the Investiture Contest*. New York, 1978.

Tellenbach, G. *Church, State and Christian Society at the Time of the Investiture Contest*. Oxford, 1940.

Tierney, B. *The Crisis of Church and State, 1050–1300*.

Toronto, 1988.
Williams, S., ed. *The Gregorian Epoch.* Boston, 1964.

The Muslims

Collins, R. *Early Medieval Spain: Unity and Diversion.* New York, 1983.
Jackson, G. *The Making of Medieval Spain.* London, 1972.
MacKay, A. *Spain in the Middle Ages. From Frontier to Empire, 1100–1500.* Basingstoke, 1977.
Russell, F. H. *The Just War in the Middle Ages.* Cambridge, 1975.
O'Callaghan, J. F. *A History of Medieval Spain.* Ithaca, 1975.
Vicens Vives, J., and J. Nadal Oller. *An Economic History of Spain.* Princeton, 1969.

The Reconquista

Brooke, R., and C. Brooke. *Popular Religion in the Middle Ages: Western Europe 1000–1300.* London, 1984.
Duby, G. *Rural Economy and Country Life in the Medieval West.* London, 1968.
Fossier, R. *Peasant Life in the Medieval West.* Oxford, 1988.
Heaton, H. *Economic History of Europe.* New York, 1948.
Hyde, J. K. *Society and Politics in Medieval Italy: The Evolution of Civil Life, 1000–1350.* London, 1973.
Postan, M. M., ed. *The Agrarian Life of the Middle Ages.* Cambridge, 1966.
White, L. *Medieval Technology and Social Change.* New York, 1966.
Wickham, C. *Early Medieval Italy: Central Power and Local Society.* London, 1981.

Byzantium

Attwater, D. *The Christian Churches of the East.* London, 1961.
Chitty, J. *The Desert: A City.* n.p., 1966.
Every, G. *The Byzantine Patriarchate.* London, 1962.
————. *Understanding Eastern Christianity.* London, 1980.
Hussey, J. M. *The Orthodox Church in the Byzantine Empire.* Oxford, 1986.
Lawrence, C. H. *Medieval Monasticism.* London/New York, 1984.
Painter, B., and S. Tierney. *Western Europe in the Middle Ages.* New York, 1985.
Rousseau, P. *Ascetics, Authority and the Church in the Age of Jerome and Cassian.* Paris, 1978.

The Middle Byzantine Empire

Hussey, J. M. *Church and Learning in the Byzantine Empire.* n.p., 1963.
Lemerle, P. *Byzantine Humanism.* Canberra, 1986.
Noble, T. F. X. *The Birth of the Papal State.* Philadelphia, 1984.
Vasiliev, A. A. *History of the Byzantine Empire.* London, 1963.
Ware, T. *The Orthodox Church.* Harmondsworth, 1963.

The Crusades

Atiya, A. S. *Crusade, Commerce and Culture.* New York, 1966.

Bradford, E. *The Great Betrayal.* London, 1967.
Mayer, H. E. *The Crusades.* London, 1972.
Powell, J. *The Anatomy of a Crusade, 1213–1221.* Philadelphia, 1977.
Prawer, J. *The Latin Kingdom of Jerusalem: European Colonialism in the Middle Ages.* London, 1972.
Queller, D. E. *The Fourth Crusade: The Conquest of Constantinople.* Leicester, 1978.
Runciman, S. *A History of the Crusades.* Cambridge, 1967.
Smail, R. C. *Crusading Warfare.* Cambridge, 1956.

Further Reading

Adams, G. B. *Civilization during the Middle Ages.* New York, 1972.
Banfield, S. *Charlemagne.* New York, 1986.
Bishop, M. *Middle Ages.* Boston, 1986.
Birt, D. *The Medieval Town.* White Plains, NY, 1974.
Cootes, R. J. *Middle Ages.* White Plains, NY, 1989.
Corbishley, M. *Middle Ages.* New York, 1990.
Davis, W. S. *Life on a Medieval Barony.* Cheshire, CT, 1990.
Duckett, E. S. *Carolingian Portraits: A Study in the Ninth Century.* Ann Arbor, 1988.
Hilton, R. H. *English and French Towns in Feudal Society: A Contemporary Study.* New York, 1992.
Jones, M. *Knights and Castles.* London, 1991.
LeGoff, J. *The Medieval Imagination.* Chicago, 1992.
McEvedy, C. *The New Penguin Atlas of Medieval History.* New York, 1992.
Mundy, J. H. *Essays in Medieval Life & Thought.* Westport, CT, 1980.
Oakley, F. *The Medieval Experience.* Toronto, 1988.
Reynolds, S. *Fiefs and Vassals: The Medieval Evidence Reinterpreted.* New York, 1994.
Rowling, M. *Everyday Life in Medieval Times.* New York, 1987.
Shahar, S. *Childhood in the Middle Ages.* New York, 1992.
Stephenson, C. *Mediaeval Feudalism.* Ithaca, 1956.

Illustration Credits

Index

Aachen *1170*, 1171, *1177*, 1183, *1185*, 1193
Abbad III al-Mutamid of Seville 1230
Abbas 1225
Abbasids, second of the two great dynasties of the Muslim Empire of the Caliphate 1225
Abbey 1160, *1161*, *1163*, 1211, *1214*, 1218, 1285
Abbot 1179, 1200, 1212, 1285, 1287
Abd al-Raḥmōn I (731-788), Umayyad emir 1225
Abd al-Raḥmōn III (889-961), Umayyad emir 1226-1230, *1162*
Acre 1278
Adelaide (931-999), consort of the Western emperor Otto I and regent for her grandson Otto III 1206, 1213, 1285, 1287
Adhemar of Le Puy, bishop (?-1098), one of the leaders of the First Crusade, Bishop of Le Puy (1077-1098) 1269
Adrian I (?-795), pope (772-795) 1166
Adrian II (792-872), pope (862-872) 1264
Adrianople 1276
Adriatic Sea 1268, 1270
Aegean Sea 1236, 1254
Aethelred the Unready (c.968-1016), Anglo-Saxon king of England (978-1016) 1193, 1206, 1286
Aethelwulf (?-858), Anglo-Saxon king of England 1193
Africa 1225, 1230, 1239-1240, 1243-1244, 1252, 1276, 1285
Agnes of Poitiers (c.1024-1077), second wife of the Holy Roman emperor Henry III and regent (1056-1062) of her son Henry IV *1220*
Agriculture 1231, 1250
Al-Nasir li-din Allah 1226-1227
Al Mawsil 1272, 1276
Al-Zahra *1227*
Al-Hakim (985-1021), sixth ruler of the Egyptian Shi'i Fatimid dynasty *1238*
Al-Kamil (1180-1238), last sultan (1218-) of the Ayyubid line 1278
Al-Hakam, caliph 1228
Albi 1277
Albigenses, heretical Christian sect in southern France (12th-13th cent.) 1277
Albigensian Crusade (1208-1213), crusade against heresy in southern France 1277
Albinus. *See* Alcuin
Alcuin (or Albinus) (735-804), Anglo-Latin poet, educator and cleric 1178-1180, 1182, 1285, *1186*
Alemanni(ans) 1162, 1167
Aleppo 1285
Alexander the Great (356-323 BC), king of Macedonia (336-323) 1286
Alexandria 1263, 1287
Alexius I Comnenus (1048-1118), Byzantine emperor (1081-1118) 1268-1269, 1272, 1274, 1285
Alfonso II the Chaste (Alfonsus Castus) (c.759-842), king of Asturias (791-842) *1234*
Alfonso III (c.838-c.910), king of Asturias (866-910) 1226, 1233-1234, *1237*
Alfonso VI (1040-1109), king of Castile and Leon 1238

Alfonso Henriques, king of Portugal (1143) 1237, 1288
Alfonsus Castus. *See* Alfonso II the Chaste
Alfred the Great (849-899), Saxon king of Wessex, England (871-899) *1193*, 1206, 1285
Alfred Jewel *1193*
Aljafaria *1228-1229*
Allah 1226
Almohads (Berber confederation that created an Islamic empire in North Africa and Spain (1130-1269) 1230, *1237*, 1237, 1239, 1285, armies *1232*, decline *1232*
Almoravids. *See* Almohads
Alp Arslan (c.1030-1072), second of the first three great sultans of the Seljuq Turks 1288
Alps 1166, 1170, 1206, 1232
Alsace 1187, 1287-1288
Amalfi 1232
Amiens 1187
Anatolia 1268-1269, 1272, 1276, 1288
Angers 1186
Angles 1285
Anglo-Saxon 1161-1162, 1164, 1178-1179, 1190, 1206, 1285-1287
Anjou 1209, 1231
Annalum Regium Francorum (Annals of the Franks) *1182*
Anthemius of Tralles (?-472), Western Roman emperor (467-472) 1251
Anti-Semitism 1270
Antioch 1263, 1272, 1274, 1276, *1276*, 1285-1287
Antrustions, member of the personal guard of the Frankish Merovingian rulers (481/2-751) 1172
Apostle Peter 1222, 1263
Apostle Paul *1168*
Apostle James *1236*
Apostolic life 1224
Apulia 1241-1242, 1270, 1288
Aquitaine 1160, 1162, 1166, 1182, 1184, 1211, 1231, 1285, 1287
Arabian Empire 1226
Arabs 1164, 1166, 1193, 1227, *1238*, 1244, *1255*, *1264*
Aragon 1233, 1236, 1239, 1285, kingdom of 1236
Aristocracy 1160, 1163, 1171, 1175, 1178, 1183, 1196, 1213, 1255. *See* also Nobility
Aristotle (384-322 BC), Greek philosopher, logician and scientist *1238*
Arithmetica 1179
Armenia 1248, 1264, 1285
Armeniakoi, regiment 1256-1257, 1259
Armenian emperors, succession of Byzantine emperors (813-842) 1285
Ascalon, Battle at (1153) 1274
Asia Minor 1244, 1259, 1264, 1266, 1268-1269, 1272, 1274, 1277-1278, 1285
Asser (?-909), Welsh monk, teacher, counsellor and biographer of Alfred the Great 1193
Astronomia 1179
Astronomy 1178-1179, 1227
Asturias, kingdom of, (718-910) independent Christian kingdom on the Iberian peninsula 1225-1226, 1230, *1231*, 1233-1234, *1234*
Athelney (878), stronghold made by king Alfred 1193
Augustine, Saint (354-430), bishop of Hippo (North Africa) 1252
Austrasia, eastern Frankish kingdom in the Merovingian period (6th-8th centuries) 1161, 1285, 1287
Austria 1167
Autonomy 1168, 1183, 1187, 1190, 1226, 1233, 1236
Avar kingdom 1167
Avars 1167, 1244
Aya Sofia. *See* Hagia Sophia

Baghdad *1174*, 1225, 1227-1228, 1250, 1288
Baldwin (Boudewijn), first count of Flanders (863-879) 1198
Baldwin of Bouillon, brother of Godfrey of Bouillon, first king of Jerusalem 1276, 1285-1286, *1274*
Baldwin of Edessa. *See* Baldwin of Bouillon
Baldwin I of Constantinople (1172-1205), count of Flanders, a leader of the Fourth crusade 1276
Baldwin I (of Jerusalem) (?1058-1118), king of the crusader state of Jerusalem (1100-1118) 1285
Baldwin II (of Jerusalem) (?-1131), king of Jerusalem (1118-1131) and crusade leader 1276, 1285
Baldwin III (1131-1162), king of Jerusalem (1143-1162) 1285
Balearic Islands 1230, 1236, 1242
Balkan Peninsula 1243
Balkans 1244, 1277
Bamberg Cathedral *1211*
Baptism 1166, by the sword 1178
Barcelona 1167, 1230, 1233, 1236
Bari 1241-1242, 1268, 1270
Basil II Bulgaroctonus (Killer of Bulgars) (c.958-1025), Byzantine emperor (963-1025) 1264-1265, *1266*, 1285
Basil I the Macedonian (?-886), Byzantine emperor (867-886) 1260, 1287
Basileus 1240, 1244-1248, 1250, 1254-1257, 1259, 1261-1264, 1266, 1268-1269, 1285
Basque 1167, 1172, 1225, 1236
Bavaria 1160, 1165, *1172*, 1178, 1202, 1213, 1286, 1288
Bavarians 1162, 1167, 1202
Belisarius (c.505-565), Byzantine general 1239
Benedict VIII (?-1024), pope (1012-1024) *1214*, 1241
Benedict IX (?-1055/1056), pope (1032-1045 and 1047-1048) 1215, 1286
Berbers 1226-1227
Berengar II (c.900-966), king of Italy (950-952) 1206, 1285
Bermudo II, king of León 1237
Bernard of Clairvaux, St. (1090-1154), Cistercian monk who summoned the French for the Second Crusade in 1146 1272, *1273*, 1285, 1288
Bishop of Rome 1164, 1166, 1206, 1222
Bishop of Bamberg 1215
Bishop 1164, 1166, 1179, *1199*, 1200, 1206, *1213*, 1215, 1222, 1227, *1236*, 1252, 1274
Bishoprics 1160, 1204-1205, 1211, 1214, 1218, 1233
Bismarck Sea 1219
Black Sea 1264
Blessing of Constantine. *See* Donatio Constantini
Blois 1186
Boethius (c.480-524), scholar, theologian, statesman and philosopher 1193
Bohemia 1213, 1286
Bohemund of Taranto (c.1050/1058-1111), one of the most important figures in the First Crusade 1270, *1276*, 1285
Boleslav I (?-967), prince of Bohemia (929-967) 1213
Bologna *1242*
Boniface (?-754), priest and missionary murdered in 754 by the Frisians 1167, *1180*
Bordeaux 1186
Boris I of Bulgaria (?-907), ruler of Bulgaria (852-889) 1264
Bosporus 1246-1247, 1272
Boudewijn of Bouillon. *See* Baldwin I of Jerusalem
Braga 1220

Text is indicated in roman type; illustrations are indicated in italic type.

Brindisi 1270
Brittany 1160, 1172
Bronze Palace 1168
Bronze Gate 1248, 1254
Bruges 1196, 1270
Bulgaria 1264, 1285, Empire 1264
Bulgaroctonos (Slayer of Bulgars).
    See Basil II
Burgos 1227
Burgundy 1187, *1194*, 1203, 1206, 1209,
    1211, 1213-1214, 1221, 1237, 1270, 1285-
    1288
Byblos *1268*
Byzantine art *1183*, 1250-1251, 1265-1266,
    church 1224, 1250, *1255*, 1263, emperor
    1164, 1168, 1180, 1208, 1222, 1244, *1248*,
    1264, 1268, 1273, 1276, 1285, 1287-1288,
    empire 1164, 1180, 1207, 1243, 1246,
    1249, *1253*, 1255, 1258-1259, 1264-1266,
    1268, 1273-1274, 1277-1278, 1285-1287,
    etiquette 1248, manuscripts *1244-1245,
    1247*, theologians 1182
Byzantines 1213, 1240-1241, 1243-1244,
    1246, *1249*, 1250, *1264*, 1264, 1268-1269,
    1272, 1274, 1288
Byzantium 1168, 1171, 1224, 1241, 1243,
    1246, 1250, 1263-1264, 1266, 1285, 1288

Cadíz 1230, 1239
Cairo 1193-1194, 1241, 1277-1278
Calabria 1241-1242, 1270, 1288
Caliph *1174*, 1194, 1226, *1227*, 1228-1229,
    1242, 1250, 1252-1253, 1259, 1266, 1285-
    1286, 1288
Caliphate of Córdoba, (929-1031) Islamic
    state in Spain *1226*, 1285, 1287-1288
Caliphate of Damascus 1225
Caliphs *1191*, 1225, 1228, 1230
Calixtus II (?-1124), pope (1119-1124) 1220,
    1285
Cambrai 1187
Canossa, 10th-century castle in Italy 1218-
    1219, 1286
Canute (Cnut) II of Denmark (c. 1043-1086),
    king of Denmark (1080-1086) 1206
Capella 1171
Capetian dynasty, ruling house of France
    (987-1328) 1285
Capitularies 1176
Cappadocia *1255, 1258*
Capua 1214, 1288
Cardeña *1240*
Cardinals 1215
Carinthia 1178, 1199
Carloman (751-771), younger brother of
    Charlemagne 1163, 1165-1166, 1191
Carolingian dynasty 1182, 1202, empire
    1175, 1182, 1287-1288, house 1183, minus-
    cule (script) 1179, *1186*, Renaissance 1178,
    1182, 1285, 1287
Carolingians 1161, 1163, 1171, 1175, 1177,
    1183, 1191-1193, 1200, 1285
Carolus. *See* Charlemagne
Castile 1227, 1230, 1233-1234, 1236-1239,
    1285, 1287-1288
Castilian culture 1285, domination 1234,
    language 1234
Castilla. *See* Castile
Castle of Canossa. *See* Canossa
Catalan Aragon 1233
Cathars 1277
Cathedral *1170, 1191, 1211, 1219, 1241*
Caucasus Mountains 1285
Cavalry 1162-1163, 1166, 1200, *1233*, 1244,
    1285
Celibacy 1200, 1216, 1263
Chalice of Ardagh *1218*
Chanson de Roland. *See* Song of Roland

Charlemagne (Charles the Great) (742-814),
    Frankish king (768-814) and Holy Roman
    emperor (800-814) 1161, *1165-1170*, 1165-
    1168, 1170-1172, *1173-1178*, 1175-1178,
    1180, 1182-1184, *1182, 1185*, 1186, 1189-
    1191, 1193-1194, 1206, 1223, 1240, 1256,
    1285-1288
Charles I. *See* Charles II
Charles II (the Bald) (823-877), Holy Roman
    Emperor (875-877), king of France as
    Charles I (843-877) 1184, *1184, 1186-1187*,
    1187, 1189-1190, 1196, *1196*, 1198, 1285,
    1287-1288
Charles the Bald. *See* Charles II
Charles the Great. *See* Charlemagne
Charles Martel (the Hammer) (c.688-741),
    ruler of the Frankish kingdom of Austrasia
    (719-741) 1161, *1162*, 1163-1164, 1178,
    1200, 1225, 1285-1287
Childeric 1287
Christendom 1168, 1171, 1177, 1213, 1233,
    1239, 1242, 1285. *See also* Christianity
Christian Church 1202, *1206*, 1224, emperor
    1182, 1246
Christianity 1161-1162, 1168, 1179, *1180*,
    1185, 1192, 1200, 1208, 1210-1211, *1218*,
    1219, 1222, 1226, 1231, 1252, *1253*, 1254,
    1262-1264, 1268, 1272
Churchright 1218, senate 1222, synods
    1179
Church of the Holy Wisdom. *See* Hagia
    Sophia
Cistercians, Roman Catholic monastic order
    (founded 1098) *1273*
Classical authors 1179, mythology *1259*
Classics 1179, 1248
Clement II (?-1047), pope (1046-1047) 1215
Clement III (c.1025-1100), antipope from
    1080 to 1100 1219, *1222*
Clergy 1171, 1178-1179, 1196, 1200, 1202,
    1204, 1209, 1218-1219, 1221, 1224, 1263
Clergymen 1161, 1179, 1215, 1224, 1254
Clerical celibacy 1216. *See also* Celibacy
Clericus 1178
Clermont. *See* Council of
Clovis I (c.466-511), founder of the Frankish
    kingdom 1287
Clunaic model 1224, pope 1268, reform
    1286
Cluny, abbey in Burgundy founded by
    William of Aquitaine in 910 1211-1212,
    1214, 1221, 1232, 1239, 1268, *1269*, 1285,
    1287
Cnut. *See* Canute
Codex Aureus, 10th century manuscript
    (Echternach) *1220, 1224*
Coimbra 1237
Comes 1175, 1234, 1237
Comitatus 1171-1172, 1174, 1185
Comitatus Portaculenis 1237
Concordat of Worms (1122), compromise
    between Pope Calixtus II and Holy Roman
    emperor Henry V on investiture 1220-1221,
    1285-1286
Conrad I of Franconia (?-918), German king
    (911-918) 1214
Conrad II of Swabia (c.990-1039), king of
    Germany (1024-1039), Holy Roman emper-
    or (1027-1039), king of the Lombards
    (1026) 1214, *1224*, 1285-1286
Conrad III (1093-1152), German king (1138-
    1152) 1272, *1273*, 1276
Conrad of Franconia. *See* Conrad II
Consolation (Consolamentum) 1277
Constantine 1168, 1170-1171, 1180, 1208,
    1212, 1245-1247, 1250, 1254, 1256-1257,
    1260-1261, *1262*, 1263-1265, 1285-1286
Constantine the Great (c.280-337), Roman
    emperor 1168, 1246, 1285-1286

Constantine IV (?-685), Byzantine emperor
    (668-685) 1170
Constantine V Copronymus (718-775),
    Byzantine emperor (741-775) 1180, 1254,
    1256-1257
Constantine VI, Byzantine emperor (780-
    797) 1180, 1256, 1285-1286
Constantine VII Porphyrogenitus (905-959),
    Byzantine emperor (908-959) 1260-1261,
    1285
Constantine VIII (c.960-1028), Byzantine co-
    ruler with Basil II (976-1025), sole ruler
    (1025-1028) 1264
Constantine IX Monomachus (1000-1055),
    Byzantine co-ruler with Zoë and Theodora
    (1042-1055) *1262*, 1263
Constantinople 1164, 1168, 1180, 1211,
    1222, 1224, 1227, 1245-1247, *1247*, 1249,
    1249-1250, 1251, 1254, 1256, 1259-1265,
    1269-1270, 1272, 1274, 1276, 1278, 1285,
    1287
Córdoba, capital of Muslim Spain (8th-11th
    cent.) 1166, *1191*, 1194, 1225, *1225-1227*,
    1227-1230, 1234, 1238, 1241, 1285-1288
Coronation 1171, 1178, 1207-1208, 1219,
    1256, 1276
Corsica 1242
Corvée 1286, 1288
Cotrone 1213
Council of Chalcedon (451), Pope Leo I tried
    to accommodate the issue of Mono-
    physitism 1250
Council of Clermont (1095), called by Pope
    Urban II to announce the First Crusade
    1267-1269, 1286, 1288
Council of lords 1164-1165
Council of Nicaea (787), ecumenical council
    of the Christian Church 1180, 1256, 1260-
    1261, 1286
Council of Orthodoxy (843), iconoclasm con-
    demned 1180, 1259
Count 1175-1176, 1183, 1196, 1198, 1211,
    1237, 1242, 1266, 1269, 1285-1286, 1288
Crete 1261, *1264*
Crusades 1267, 1278, *1278*
Cyprus 1278
Cyril, Saint (375-444), theologian and bishop
    1264
Cyrillic alphabet 1264

Dagobert I (605-639), last Frankish king of
    the Merovingian dynasty *1160-1161, 1163*
Damascus 1225-1226, 1263, 1273, 1276,
    1285-1286, 1288
Damietta 1277-1278
Danegeld 1206
Danelaw 1206, 1286
Danish March 1287
Danube 1287
Daphni *1263*
De Administrando Imperio 1261
De Ceremoniis Aulae Byzantinae 1261
De Germania 1171
De Thematibus 1261
Denmark 1186, 1206, 1287
Desiderius (ruled 757-774), Lombard ruler of
    Italy 1166
Deus le vult 1267, 1269
Dialectica. *See* Dialectics
Dialectics 1179
Dictionaries 1179
Diet of Würzburg (1121), Henry V's peace
    with princes and papacy ending the German
    civil wars 1220
Diocletian's Edict (301) 1249
Direct taxation 1206
Dokkum *1180*
Donatio Constantini, document concerning
    the supposed grant by Constantine the Great

to Pope Sylvester I (314-335) 1168, 1208, 1212, 1286

Donation of Pépin (754), king Pépin III's promise to win lands in Italy for Pope Stephen II 1288

Dormitorium *1214*

Donation of Constantine. *See* Donatio Constantini

Donation 1168, 1208, 1212, 1286, 1288

Dorylaeum 1272

Drang nach Osten 1233

Dublin 1206

Duke of Bavaria 1213

Duke of Normandy 1286

Durandel 1172

Easter 1166, 1179, 1266

Eastern Roman Empire 1239

Eastern (Orthodox) church 1250, 1252, 1263

Ebro 1168

Ecclesiastical symbols 1221

Ecloga, compilation of Byzantine law issued in 726 by Emperor Leo III the Isaurian 1255

Edessa 1272-1274, 1276, 1285-1286, 1288

Egypt 1243-1244, 1250, 1263, 1273, 1276-1277, 1286

Eikon 1180, 1252, 1286

Einhard (c.770-840), Frankish scholar and monk, biographer of Charlemagne 1170, 1172, 1182, *1182*, 1286

El Cid Campeador (The Lord Champion) (c.1040-1099), born Rodrigo Díaz de Vivar, Spanish legendary warrior 1237, 1239, *1240*, 1286

El cantar de mío Cid 1238

Elbe 1168, 1206, 1233

Emir 1194, 1225-1226, 1242, 1274

Emissary counts *1286*

England 1179, 1193, 1206, 1221, 1285-1287

Epistula de litteris colendis 1179

Estremadura 1230, 1234

Eucharist 1263

Eunuch 1228, 1256

Europe 1159, 1166, 1168, *1174*, *1179-1180*, 1182, 1185, *1188*, *1190*, 1192, 1196, 1200-1202, *1202*, 1206, *1207*, 1210-1212, 1227, 1231, *1238*, *1242*, 1242-1244, 1246, 1261, 1264-1265, 1269, 1272-1274, 1276-1278, 1285-1287

Excommunication 1218-1220, 1263, 1287

Fatimids, Muslim dynasty ruling in North Africa and the Middle East (909-1171) 1193, 1226

Ferdinand I (c.1016/1018-1065), king of Castile (1033-), king of León (1037-), emperor of Spain (1056-) 1234, 1237-1238

Ferdinand III (the Saint) (?1201-1252), king of Castile (1217-1252) and León (1230-1252) 1234

Fernán González, Count, declared himself first king of Castile in 932 1227

Feudal system 1163, 1174-1175, 1209

Feudalism 1189, 1200-1202, 1210, 1232, 1250, 1286, 1288

Feurs *1189*

Fiefdom 1162-1164, 1174-1175, 1210

Fifth Crusade (1217-1221) 1277

First Crusade (1096-1099), under Godfrey of Bouillon and Raymond of Toulouse 1269, *1269-1270*, 1272, 1276, *1278*, 1285-1288

Flanders 1187, 1196, 1198, 1231, 1270, 1285-1286

Fontenay, Battle at (841), Lothar I battled against his brothers Louis the German and Charles the Bald 1187, 1287-1288

Fourth Crusade (1202-1204) 1276-1277

France *1163*, *1174*, 1187, *1189*, 1206, 1209-1211, 1213, 1221, 1225, 1236, 1268, 1270,

1273, 1273-1274, 1276-1278, 1285, 1287

Franconia. *See* Franks

Franconian dynasty 1214, 1221

Frankish Empire 1159-1160, 1163, 1171, 1182, 1193-1194, 1196, 1199, 1202, *1202*, *1206*, 1231, 1286-1287, law 1159, rule 1178

Franks 1161, 1163, 1165-1166, 1168, 1171, 1175-1176, 1178, 1182, *1182*, 1186, 1191, 1193, 1202-1203, 1227, 1239, 1272, 1286-1288

Frederick I Barbarossa (c.1123-1190), Holy Roman emperor (1155-1190) 1276

Frederick II (1194-1250), Holy Roman emperor (1120-), king of Germany and Sicily 1277

Friesland 1187

Frisians 1161-1162, 1167, 1176, *1180*, 1286

Galicia 1226, 1230, 1234

Gau 1175-1176, 1187, 1286

Gaul 1174, 1187, 1194, 1287

Gautier Sans-Avoir. *See* Walter the Penniless

Gelasius II (?-1119), pope (1118-1119) 1220

Genoa 1242, 1274

Geometry (*Geometria*) 1179

Gerbert. *See* Sylvester II

Germanic tribes 1167

Germany 1162, *1170*, 1171, 1187, 1191, 1204, 1206, *1211*, 1213-1214, *1216*, 1219, *1222*, 1224, 1231, 1272, 1276, 1285-1287

Ghetto 1270

Godfrey of Bouillon (1060-1100), duke of Lower Lotharingia and a leader of the First Crusade *1267*, 1270, 1274, 1285-1286

Golden Book or Gospels *1220*, *1224*

Goths 1168

Gotland *1188*

Graeci 1244

Grammar 1179

Grammatica 1179

Granada 1230, 1238, 1286

Great Britain 1193, *1194*

Great Schism, the (1054) 1222, 1224, 1263, 1287

Greece *1251*, *1257*, *1263*, 1264, 1268, 1277, 1286

Greek 1178, 1180, *1197*, 1227, *1238*, 1240, *1240*, 1243-1244, 1248, 1252, 1254, 1263, 1265-1266, 1269, 1272, 1286, philosophers 1227

Greenland 1206, 1287

Gregorian Reform (1073) 1215, 1286

Gregory I (c.540-604), pope (590-604) 1193, 1213, 1219, 1221-1222, *1221-1222*, 1268, 1273, 1276, 1278, 1286

Gregory VI (?-1048), pope (1045-1046) 1215, 1286

Gregory VII (St. Hildebrand, born Odo of Lagery) (c.1020-1085), pope (1073-1085) 1215, 1219, 1221, *1222*, 1232, 1268, 1286

Gregory VIII (?-c.1137), antipope (1118-1121) 1220-1221, 1273, 1276

Gregory IX (c.1170-1241), pope (1227-1241) 1278

Grenada 1239

Guibert of Ravenna. *See* Clement III

Hagia Sophia (St. Sophia, Church of the Holy Wisdom) *1243*, 1247, *1251*, *1260*, 1263, 1266, 1274

Hagib 1228-1230, 1238, 1286

Halab 1272, 1276

Hammam *1239*

Harley Gospels *1180*

Hārūn al Rashīd (c.766-809), fifth caliph of the Abbasid dynasty *1174*

Hebrides 1206

Henry of Bavaria. *See* Henry II

Henry of Burgundy, Count of Portugal (12th century) 1237, 1288

Henry the Fowler. *See* Henry I

Henry the Saint. *See* Henry II

Henry I (the Fowler) of Saxony (876?-939), German king (925-939) 1202, 1221, 1286-1287

Henry II (the Saint) of Bavaria (973-1024), king of Germany (1002-1024), king of the Lombards (1004-1024) and Holy Roman emperor (1014-1024) *1211*, 1213, 1286

Henry III the Black (1017–1056), king of Germany (1028–1056) and Holy Roman emperor (1039–1056) 1214-1215, *1220*, 1286

Henry IV (1050-1106), king of Germany (1056-1106) and Holy Roman emperor (1084-1106) 1215-1216, 1218-1219, *1221-1222*, 1286-1287

Henry V (1086-1125), German king and Holy Roman emperor 1219-1221, 1285

Heraclius (c.575-641), Eastern Roman emperor 1244, 1246, 1248

Hiera 1180

Hieria 1254

Hildebrand, hero of song of Hildebrand (Hildebrandslied) 1215, 1218, 1224, 1286

Hildebrand, Saint. *See* Gregory VII

Hildesheim *1219*

Hippocrates (c.460-c.377 BC), Greek physician *1238*

Hippodrome 1249

Hisham II, Hisham ibn'abd al-Malik (691-743), tenth caliph *1227*

Hisham III (?-1036), last Umayyad 1230

Historia Roderici 1238

History 1163, 1166-1168, 1171, 1178-1179, 1182, 1198, 1211, 1219, 1233, 1250, 1261, 1266, 1270, 1276

Holy City 1276

Holy Communion 1224

Holy Father 1241

Holy Land 1267-1268, *1272*, 1273, 1277-1278, *1278*, 1286

Holy mass 1179

Holy Roman emperors 1191, 1202, 1206, 1213-1215, 1219, 1231, 1242, 1264, 1272, 1276-1277, 1285-1288

Holy Roman Empire *1165*, 1171, 1177, 1192, 1213, *1215*, 1216, 1256, 1285-1286

Holy Spirit 1223, 1266

Holy war 1230

Hruodlandus 1172

Humbert (c.1000-1061), theologian and papal legate 1263

Hungary 1167, 1270

Iberian Muslims 1227, 1233-1234

Iberian peninsula 1225-1226, 1233-1234, 1238

Iconoclasm 1168, 1180, 1252-1256, *1256*, *1258*, 1259, *1262*, 1286-1287

Iconoclasts 1180, 1252, 1254

Iconodouloi 1252, 1254, 1286, rulers 1257

Icons 1180, 1250, 1252-1256, 1259, *1261*, 1265, 1286, 1288

Idolatry 1180, 1254

Imad ad-Din Zangi. *See* Zangi

Immunity (*Immunitas*) 1183-1184, 1286

Innocent III (1160/1161-1216), pope (1198-1216) 1277

Inquisition 1236

Investiture controversy, power struggle between papacy and Holy Roman Empire (11th-12th cent.) 1215-1216, 1218-1221, 1224, 1285-1286

Investiture debate 1221

Iran *1174*

Text is indicated in roman type; illustrations are indicated in italic type.

1293

Ireland 1192, 1206, *1218*

Irene (752-803), Byzantine empress (797-802), married to Emperor Leo IV in 769 and regent for her son Constantine VI (780-790 and 792-797) 1170-1171, 1180, 1255-1256, 1285-1287

Isaac I Comnenus (c.1005-1061), Byzantine emperor (1057-1059) 1269

Isaac II Angelus (c.1135-1204), Byzantine emperor (1185-1204) 1276

Isabel of Castile (1451-1504), queen of Castile and Aragon 1236

Isaurian dynasty, founded by Leo III the Isaurian (Byzantine Empire, 717-802) 1255-1256, 1286

Isidorus of Miletus, architect 1251

Islam 1226-1227, *1229*, *1238*, 1288

Islamic civilization 1226, culture 1227, 1241-1242, 1259, 1288, world *1174*, 1230, *1242*

Istanbul *1243*

Italy 1162, 1164, 1166, 1168, 1170-1171, 1179, 1183, 1187-1188, 1191, 1193-1194, 1205-1207, 1212-1214, 1218, *1218*, 1221, 1231, 1233, 1239-1244, *1242*, 1251, 1254, 1263, 1269-1270, 1272, 1277-1278, 1286-1288

Jaén 1230, 1234

Jerome, Saint, Church father *1178*

Jerusalem 1263, 1267, *1267*, 1269, 1272-1274, *1274*, 1276, 1278, 1285-1288

Jews 1227, 1230, 1270, 1272, 1287

Jihad 1230

John XII (c.937-964), pope (955-964) 1206, 1208, 1231, 1240, 1287

John of Brienne (c.1148-1237), count of Brienne, king of Jerusalem, Latin emperor of Constantinople 1276

John Orphanotropus, eunuch who governed the Byzantine Empire (1034-1042) 1287

John Scotus Erigena, Irish theologian 1193

John I Tzimisces (925-976), Byzantine emperor (969-976) 1264

Jordan River 1274

Justinian I, Flavius Petrus Sabbatius Justinianus (483-565), Byzantine emperor (527-565) 1239, *1243-1244*, 1243, 1251, 1266

Justinian II, Eastern Roman emperor (527-565) *1244*

Jutes 1285

Kadi 1228, 1287

Khan Krum, reigned Lower Mousia from 803 to 814 1264

Kiev *1253*

Kloein 1180, 1252, 1286

Koran 1227, 1253

Krak des Chevaliers, castle *1278*

Kunigunde, wife of Henry II *1211*

La Mezquita 1228

Labors of Hercules *1259*

Landowners 1160, 1174, 1183, 1187, 1190, 1196, 1218, 1250, 1254, 1265, 1286

Las Navas de Tolosa, Battle at (1212) *1232*

Lateran Palace (Rome) 1215

Lebanon *1268*, *1277*

Lechfield, Battle at (955), king Otto I the Great defeated the Magyars 1231

Leo I the Great, Saint (?-461), pope (440-461) 1250

Leo III the Isaurean (c.675/680-741), Byzantine emperor (717-741) and founder of the Isaurian dynasty 1180, 1254-1256, *1256*, 1259, 1286-1287

Leo III, Saint (?-816), pope (795-816) *1165*, *1168*, 1170, *1170*, 1287

Leo IV (749-780), Byzantine emperor 1255-1256, 1285-1286

Leo IV, Saint (?-855), pope (847-855) 1240

Leo V the Armenian (?-820), Byzantine emperor (813-820) 1257-1258, *1261-1262*, 1285, 1287

Leo VI (866-912), Byzantine co-emperor from 870 and emperor from 886 to 912 1260

Leo VIII (?-965), pope (963-965) 1206, 1287

Leo IX, Saint (1002-1054), pope (1049-1054) 1287

León 1226-1227, 1230, 1233-1234, 1236-1237, 1285, 1287

Levant 1276

Liberal arts 1179, 1227

Library 1178-1179

Libri Carolini, treatise (c.791) in the name of Charlemagne 1180

Life of Charlemagne 1182

Limerick 1206

Lindisfarne 1206

Lisbon 1230, 1237-1238

Livy, Titus Livius (59/64 BC-17 AD), Roman historian 1179

Loire 1161, 1186, *1189*

Lombard kingdom 1166

Lombards, Germanic people who ruled a kingdom in Italy (568-774) 1164-1166, 1168, 1170, 1175-1176, 1179, 1213-1214, 1239, 1244, 1285-1288

Lombardy 1178, 1206, 1213, 1285, 1287

London 1193

Lope de Vega (1562-1635), Spanish dramatist 1238

Lorraine 1187, 1199, 1202-1203, 1213-1214, 1270, 1286-1288

Lothar I (795-855), Frankish emperor 1182, 1184, *1184*, *1186*, 1187, 1190, 1199, 1213, 1287-1288

Lotharingia. *See* Lorraine

Louis the Child (893-911), king of Germany (899-911) 1202

Louis I the Pious (778-840), Holy Roman emperor (814-840), king of France (814-840), king of Germany (814-840) and king of Aquitaine (781-840) 1285, 1287

Louis II the German (c. 806-876), king of Germany (840-876) 1184, 1187, 1190-1191, 1199, 1240, 1286-1288

Louis VI (1081-1137), king of France (1108-1137) 1221

Louis VII (1120-1180), Capetian king of France 1273, *1273*, 1276

Louis IX of France (1214-1270) (also Saint Louis), king of France (1248-1270) 1278

Low Countries 1287-1288. *See also* Netherlands

Lower Moesia 1264

Lowlands 1187

Ludwig. *See* Louis

Lyon 1270

Macedonia 1260, 1264

Macedonian dynasty 1259-1260, 1265, 1285, Renaissance 1265

Macedonians, dynasty of Byzantine emperors (842-1025) 1287

Magyars *1190*, 1193, 1202-1204, 1206, 1231, 1264, 1287

Mahdi 1230

Maior domus (Mayor of the palace) 1160-1161, 1287

Majordomo. *See* Maior domus

Malik Shah (1055-1092), third Seljuq sultan 1288

Mameluke dynasty, ruled Egypt and Syria (1250-1517) 1278

Manuscript *1159*, *1162*, *1173*, *1177*, 1179, *1180*, *1197*, *1199*, *1223*, *1233*, *1238*, *1244-1245*, *1247*, 1261, *1269*

Manzikert, Battle at (1072), marking the end of Byzantine imperial power in Asia Minor 1266, 1268, 1285, 1288

Margrave (marquise) 1287

Marrakesh *1237*

Mathematics 1178, 1227, 1261

Matthew, Saint, the Evangelist, one of the 12 apostles 1222, 1263

Maurice Bourdin, archbishop of Braga, later antipope Gregory VIII 1220

Mauricius, Flavius Tiberius (c. 539-602), general and Byzantine emperor (582-602) 1244

Mayor of the palace. *See* Maior domus

Mayoral dynasty. *See also* Carolingians 1161

Mecca 1226-1227, 1288

Mediterranean 1193, 1227, 1232-1233, 1236, 1242-1244, 1264, 1273, 1276, 1278, 1288

Meerssen, Treaty of (870), divided the northern part of Lothar I's empire between Charles the Bald and Louis the German 1199, 1288

Mercia 1287

Meroveus (c.450), king of the Salian Franks 1287

Merovingian Empire 1178, 1285, 1287

Merovingian dynasty, Frankish rule, centered in Gaul (476-751) 1159

Merovingians 1162-1163, 1178, 1183, 1287

Mesopotamia 1244, 1250, 1261, 1264

Meteora *1251*

Methodius of Olympus (?-311), early Christian cleryman 1264

Michael I Cerularius, patriarch of Constantinople (1043 to 1057) 1263, 1287

Michael II (?-829), Byzantine emperor (820-829) 1259, *1259*, 1287-1288

Michael III (838-867), Byzantine emperor 1259, 1264

Michael IV (?-1041), Byzantine emperor 1263, 1265, 1287

Michael V Caliphates (?-1042), Byzantine emperor (1041-1042) 1287

Michael VIII Palaeologus (1224-1282), Byzantine emperor (1259-1282) 1277

Middle East 1267, 1278, 1288

Middle Ages 1159, 1168, 1172, 1218, 1231, 1234, 1236, 1240, 1277

Mikligardr 1246

Minarets 1225, *1243*

Mohammed (Muhammad) (c. 570-632), founder of the religion of Islam 1194, 1225, 1227, 1230

Mohammedans *1162*, *1167*

Monastery of San Pedro *1240*

Monetary system 1250

Monophysitism 1250

Moors 1225, 1240, 1288

Moroccan Atlas mountains 1230

Morocco 1226, *1237*

Muezzin 1225

Murcia 1230, 1239

Muslim dynasty 1288

Muslims 1162, 1164, 1172, 1194, 1213, 1225, 1227, 1230, 1233-1234, 1237-1242, *1239*, 1262, 1264, 1270, 1272, 1274, 1276, 1278, 1285-1288

Mustasib 1228, 1287

Nantes 1186

Naples 1213, 1236, 1244, 1288

Narbonne *1162*

Navarre 1227, 1233-1234, 1287

Navas de Tolosa, Battle of (1212), major battle of the Christian reconquest of Spain *1232*, 1237

Netherlands *1180. See also* Low Countries

Neustria 1161, 1287

Nicaea, Empire of, founded in 1204 by Theodore I Lascaris as an independent principality of the fragmented Byzantine Empire 1268, 1272

Nicaea. *See* Council of Nicaea

Nicephorus I (?-811), Byzantine emperor (802-811) 1171, 1256, 1286

Nicephorus II Phocas (912-969), Byzantine emperor (963-969) 1261-1262, 1264, *1264*

Nile 1278

Nithard (?790-844), Frankish count and historian 1182, 1287

Nobility 1171-1172, 1175, 1190, 1196, 1198, 1200, 1202-1204, 1209-1210, 1214-1215, 1218, 1224, 1232, 1237, 1286, 1288. *See also* Aristocracy

Nomisma. *See* Solidus

Nordic people 1206, 1287

Normands 1184

Normandy 1193, 1209, 1231, 1286-1287

Normans 1184, 1186-1187, 1192-1193, 1197-1199, 1206, *1207*, 1219, *1222*, *1241*, 1241-1242, 1263, 1268, 1287-1288

North Africa 1225, 1230, 1239, 1243, 1252, 1285

North Sea 1206, 1286, empire 1206

North America 1287

Northmen. *See* Normans

Norway 1186, 1206, *1207*

Nova Roma 1285

Nur ad-Din (1118-1174), Muslim ruler 1276, 1285

Oath of Allegiance 1171, 1174-1176, 1190, 1229, 1242, 1272

Oaths of Strasbourg (oaths of Alliance sworn in 842 by Charles the Bald and Louis the German against Lothar I) *1186,* 1187, 1287

Oder 1233

Odo of Lagery. *See* Gregory VII

Odo (Eudes), Saint (c. 879–944), Cluny abbot 1192, 1209, 1211-1212, 1224, 1287

Offa (?-796), king in early Anglo-Saxon England (757-796) 1287

Old Testament 1164, 1251, 1277

Old Church Slavonic 1264

Old High German 1178

Ordoño II, king of Asturias (9th cent) *1234*

Orient 1227

Orkney Islands *1194*

Orléans 1186, 1209

Orthodoxy 1180, 1259, 1263-1264, 1266

Otto I the Great (912-973), German king and Holy Roman emperor (962-973) *1201,* 1204, *1204,* 1206, 1208, 1213-1214, 1240, 1285-1287

Otto II (955-983), German king (961-983), Holy Roman emperor (967-983) 1208, 1213, *1216,* 1264

Otto III (980-1002), German king and Holy Roman emperor *1170,* 1213, *1216,* 1286

Ottoman Turks 1277

Outremer, Near Eastern crusader states (12th-13th cent.) 1290

Oxford *1242*

Paderborn 1166

Padua *1242*

Pagus 1175

Palaeologan dynasty, prominent Byzantine family (11th cent.) 1277

Pale Death 1262

Palermo 1194, *1240-1241,* 1241-1242

Palestine 1243, 1268-1269, *1270,* 1273, *1274,* 1278, 1287-1288

Pamplona *1167*

Papacy 1164, 1168, 1206, 1209, 1211, 1215, 1220-1222, 1224, 1231, 1263, 1286-1287. *See also* Pontificate

Papal vassal 1242

Papal Power 1213

Papal States 1178, 1288

Paris 1159, 1186, 1209, 1213, *1242,* 1270

Parish school 1179

Paschal II (?-1118), pope (1099-1118) 1219

Pastoral Care 1193

Patriarch 1211, 1224, 1245, 1250, 1254, 1262-1263, *1264,* 1287

Patriarchate (Constantinople) 1221

Paul, apostle. *See* Saint Paul

Paulus Diaconus 1179

Paulus Orosius 1193

Pavia 1164, 1166

Peace of God 1232-1233, 1287

Peasants' Crusade 1269

Pecheneg Turks, nomadic Turkish people north of the Black Sea (6th-12th cent.) 1269

Pelayo (?-c.737), first king of the Christian kingdom of Asturias 1226

Pentecost 1266

Pépin of Herstal (c. 635-c.714), mayor of the palace of Austrasia *1160,* 1161, 1285, 1287

Pépin II of Aquitaine (?-c. 864), Carolingian king of Aquitane 1184, 1287

Pépin the Short (c.714-768), mayor of the palace of Austrasia (741-751) and king of the Franks (751-768) *1159, 1161-1162,* 1240, 1287

Persia 1244, 1288

Peter, apostle. *See* Saint Peter

Peter the Hermit (c. 1050-1115), ascetic, monastic founder, crusader and preacher 1269, 1287

Philip I (1052-1108), king of France from 1060 1274

Philip II Augustus, of France (1165-1223), first Capetian king of France 1276

Phocas (?-610), Byzantine emperor (602-610) 1244, 1246, 1261, 1264, 1287

Pisa 1242

Plague 1248

Plato (c. 428-348/347 BC), Greek philosopher *1238*

Poetry 1179, 1182

Poitiers, Agnes of, wife of Henry III *1120*

Poitiers, Battle of (732) 1163

Poland 1213

Pompey the Great, Gnaeus Pompeius Magus (106-48 BC), Roman statesman and general (late Roman Republic) 1286

Pontificate 1219. *See also* Papacy

Pope 1168, 1180, 1184, 1221, 1250, 1254

Portugal 1234, 1236-1237, 1288

Principate 1183

Prophet Muhammad. *See* Mohammed

Protector of the Holy Sepulchre 1276

Psalm singing 1179

Pyramid 1196, 1202, 1221

Pyrenees 1162, 1167, 1172, 1206, 1225, 1234, 1285, 1287

Quierzy-sur-Oise 1188

Ravenna 1168, *1170,* 1171, 1219, 1239, 1244, 1251, 1288

Raymond of Toulouse (1042-1105), one of the leaders in the First Crusade 1270, 1274, 1286, 1288

Reconquista 1227, *1229,* 1231, *1231,* 1234, 1237, 1239, *1239-1240,* 1288

Refectorium *1214*

Reform movement 1212, 1224, 1230, 1239

Reformation movements 1232

Reichenau *1186, 1222*

Reims 1187, 1200

Renaissance 1175, 1178, 1182, 1261

Rhetorica 1179

Rhine 1162, 1166, 1187, 1197

Rhineland 1270

Rhodes 1278

Richard I the Lion-Heart, of England (1157-1199), king of England (1189-1199) 1276

Richard II (1367-1400), king of England (1377-1399) 1286

Río Barbate, Battle at (711), Roderick defeated the Berbers 1226

Robert I of Flanders (c. 1031-1093), count of Flanders (1071-1093) 1270

Robert the Bold, Norman count 1187, 1192, 1209

Robert Guiscard (c. 1015-1085), military adventurer 1219, 1242, 1268, 1270

Roderick (?-711), Visigoth king 1226

Rodrigo Diaz de Vivar. *See* El Cid

Roger I (c.1031-1101), Norman conquerer of Sicily 1242, 1288

Roger II (1095-1154), first king of Sicily (1130-1154) 1242, 1288

Roland. *See* Song of Roland

Romaioi 1244

Roman church 1224, 1263

Roman clergymen 1215

Roman Empire *1165,* 1168, 1171-1172, 1177, 1192, 1213, *1215,* 1216, *1218,* 1239, *1242,* 1243, 1246, 1256, 1285-1287

Roman law 1183

Roman students 1179

Roman Synod of 1075 1216

Romanus I, Byzantine co-emperor 1261

Romanus II (939-963), Byzantine emperor (959-963) 1208, 1261, 1264, *1265*

Romanus III, prefect of Constantinople (11th cent.) 1265

Romanus IV Diogenes, Byzantine emperor (1068-1071) 1266, 1288

Rome 1164, 1166, 1168, *1168,* 1170-1171, 1178, 1180, 1184, 1187, 1191, 1193-1194, 1206, *1208,* 1212-1215, *1216,* 1219-1223, 1226, 1240, 1244, 1249-1250, 1254, 1263, 1285, 1287

Roncesvalles, Battle at (788), massacre by the Basques of the rear guard of Charlemagne's army in the Pyrenees Mountains 1172, *1173*

Ronda *1239*

Rouen 1186

Rudolf III, king of Burgundy (11th cent.) 1213-1214

Rudolf, duke of Swabia (?-1080) 1219

Rumania *1252*

Runic characters *1188*

Russia 1261

Sahara 1285

Saladin, sultan 1273, 1276

Salerno 1213-1214, 1219, 1232, *1242*

Salian dynasty. *See* Franconian dynasty

Salic law (*Lex Salica*), code of the Salian Franks, issued c. 507/511 1184

San Vitale *1170,* 1251

Sancho I (?-925), king of Navarre from 905 1227

Sancho II of Castile (c. 1038-1072), king of Castile from 1065 1237

Sancho III (c. 992-1035), king of Navarre (1000-1035) 1234

Santa Maria Maggiore 1215

Santiago de Compostela *1236*

Saracens 1193, 1240, 1288

Saragossa 1167, 1230, 1238-1239

Sardinia 1236, 1242-1243

Saxon rulers 1213

Saxons 1162, 1166-1167, 1175-1176, 1178, 1193, 1202, 1285

Saxony 1178, 1202-1203, 1209, 1214, 1216, 1286, 1288

Text is indicated in roman type; illustrations are indicated in italic type.

Scandinavia 1185, 1206
Schism 1211, 1224, 1268-1269
Scotland 1206
Second Crusade (1147-1149) 1272-1273, *1273*, 1276, 1285-1286, 1288
Secular nobility 1224, 1286
Secular regalia 1221
Seine 1186-1187, 1193, Valley 1187, 1193
Seleucid Kingdom (312-64 BC), Hellenistic state centered in Syria 1286
Seleucus I Nicator (358/354-281 BC), founder of the Seleucid Kingdom 1285
Seljuk realm 1276
Seljuk Turks 1266, 1268-1269, 1272, 1288
Serbia 1264
Seville 1230, *1226*, 1234, 1239
Shipyard *1249*
Sicily 1168, 1193-1194, 1236, *1240*, 1240-1243, *1264*, 1269, 1287-1288
Sidon, castle of *1277*
Simony 1211, 1215-1216, 1287-1288
Sjavidarsund 1246
Slavs 1202, 1233, 1264
Soissons 1187
Solidus 1168, 1250
Somme 1187
Song of Roland (*Chanson de Roland*) 1167, 1172, *1173*, 1288
Sophia 1264
Souks 1227
Spain 1162, 1166, *1167*, 1172, 1174, 1179, *1191*, 1194, 1206, 1223, 1225, 1230, 1233-1234, 1236, *1236*, 1238-1240, *1238-1240*, 1242-1243, 1285-1288
Spanish March 1178
Spoleto 1178
Saint Denis *1161*, *1163*
Saint John Lateran *1168*
Saint Paul *1214*
Saint Peter 1170, *1214*
Saint Peter's Basilica 1166, 1170
Saint Sophia *1243*. *See also* Hagia Sophia
Stauracius 1256
Stephen II (?-757), pope from 752 to 757 1164, 1288
Strait of Gibraltar 1225
Stratégos 1248
Suetonius, Gaius Suetonius Tranquillus (69-c. 122), Roman biographer 1179, 1182
Suzdal *1253*
Swabia 1202, 1219, 1285-1286, 1288
Sweden 1186
Swedes 1206, 1287
Sylvester II (c. 945-1003), head of the Roman Catholic Church (999-1003) 1213
Sylvester III (?-c. 1046), pope (1045) 1215
Synod 1218, 1263
Syria 1244, 1250, 1261, 1263-1264, 1268-1269, 1272, 1278, *1278*, 1285-1286, 1288

Tacitus, Cornelius (56-c. 120), Roman orator and public official 1171
Tagmata 1248
Tagus River 1237
Tancred de Hauteville (?-1112), one of the leaders of the First Crusade 1242
Taranto 1213, 1270, *1276*, 1285
Tariq ibn-Ziyad (?-720), general who led the first Muslim invasion of Spain (711) 1225
Tassilo III of Bavaria, Duke 1165, 1167, *1172*
Tax collection 1250
Tax system 1228
Taxes 1206, 1228, 1249-1250, 1256, 1262
Templars *1277*
Tenant farmers 1160, 1196, 1227
Tessarakontapechys 1253
Testry, Battle at (687) 1161
Textile production 1232
Themata (themes) 1248

Theocracy 1221
Theodomiro, first Bishop of Santiago de Compostela *1236*
Theodora (c. 500-548), Byzantine empress, wife of the emperor Justinian I (527-565) 1243, 1251, 1259
Theodosius III (?-717), Byzantine emperor (715-717) 1254, 1287
Theodulf (750-821), prelate, poet, and theologian 1179
Theology 1168, 1178, 1211, 1248, 1250, 1266
Theophano (c. 956-991), Byzantine empress 1208, 1213, 1261-1262
Theophilus (?-842), Eastern Roman emperor (829-842) 1259
Thera *1254*
Third Crusade (1187-1192) 1273, 1276, 1286
Thomas the Slav (?-823), a Slavic officer 1259, 1288
Thrace 1264
Thuringians 1162, 1167
Tiglath-pileser III, king of Assyria (744-727 BC) 1286
Tigris River 1276
Togrul Beg 1288
Toledo 1227, 1230, 1239
Toll collection 1198
Toll rights 1184
Toulouse 1226, 1270, 1274, 1286, 1288
Tours 1179, 1186, *1187*, 1285
Tribal dukedoms 1286, 1288
Trier *1216*
Tripoli 1276, 1286
Tritheists 1250
Trustis (Trust of Warriors) 1172
Tunis 1278
Tunisia 1278

Umayyads 1166, 1194, 1225-1226, 1228, 1230, 1252, 1288
Urban II (1040-1099), pope (1088-1099) 1267-1269, *1269*, 1285-1286, 1288
Utrecht 1161, 1221

Valencia 1230, 1236, 1238-1239
Valhalla *1188*
Vassals (Vassi) 1174-1175, 1190, 1201, 1209-1210, 1214, 1232, 1286, 1288
Venice 1171, 1232, 1278
Verdun, Treaty of (843), divided up the Carolingian Empire between Charles the Bald, Louis the German and Lothar I 1187, 1287-1288
Viking ship 1206, *1207*
Vikings 1175, 1184, 1186-1187, 1191-1192, 1206, 1246, 1285-1287
Virgil (Publius Vergilius Maro) (70-21 BC), Roman poet 1179
Visigoth kingdom 1225
Visigoths 1226-1227, 1285
Vizier 1228, 1230
Voronet *1252*

Waddenzee 1286
Walter the Penniless (?-1097), French knight, a leader of the Peasants' Crusade 1269, 1287
Warships *1249*
Waterford 1206
Wessex 1193, 1206
Western Roman Catholic church 1263
Western Europe 1159, *1174*, *1180*, *1188*, *1190*, 1287
Western Empire 1177
Wexford 1206
Wicklow 1206
Widukind (10th cent.), Saxon monk and historian 1166

William the Conqueror (c. 1028-1087), duke of Normandy (1035-1087), king of England (1066-1087) 1287
William of Aquitaine, West Frankish count (10th cent.), founded Cluny abbey in 910 1211, 1285
Worms, Concordat of (1122) 1220-1221, 1285-1286
Worms, Council of (1076), Henry IV deposed the pope 1218

Yazid I (c. 645-683), second Umayyad Caliph (680-683) 1252-1253
York 1206
Yusuf (?-1106), one of the major rulers of the Almoravids (reigned 1061-1106) 1225

Zacharias, Saint (?-752), pope (741-752) 1163-1164
Zangi (Imad-ad-Din-Zangi) (Zengi) (1084-1146), Iraqi ruler who founded the Zangid dynasty and fought against the crusader kingdoms in the Middle East 1272, 1276
Zoë (906-c. 920), Byzantine empress, wife of Leo VI 1265, 1287
Zwentibold (?-900), king of a heathland near Susteren, illegitimate son of Arnulf 1196, 1199-1200

Text is indicated in roman type; illustrations are indicated in italic type.